#1
THE ACCLAIMED
NATIONAL BESTSELLER!

"POIGNANT, ABSORBING
AND (SURELY NO SURPRISE) ENTERTAINING...
Genuinely funny and not infrequently hilarious...
Punctuated with far too much wit, hope and
positive thinking to be labeled a tragedy."
New York Daily News

"INTIMATE,
disturbingly raw and riotously funny in parts...
The book reads as though she's sitting right there
across from you, doing what she did best:
telling an awfully funny story
that was both truthful and shocking."
Denver Post

"TOUCHING AND WITTY"
USA Today

"GUTSY, INSPIRATIONAL, FUNNY,
smartly written and—in the end—incredibly sad...
Radner's refusal to abandon her search
for happiness, laughter and life
makes the book a fine gift for anyone."
Pittsburgh Post-Gazette

"SURPRISING...UPLIFTING...
A STORY OF TRIUMPH"
Greensboro News & Record

GILDA RADNER

IT'S ALWAYS SOMETHING

AVON BOOKS ◆ NEW YORK

To my dear husband,
Gene Wilder

Grateful acknowledgment is made to Charles E. Tuttle Co., Inc., for permission to quote from *Zen Flesh, Zen Bones* by Paul Reps.

Every effort has been made by Simon & Schuster to trace the ownership of all copyrighted material in the picture section. In the event of any question arising as to the use of any material, the editor and publisher, while expressing regret for any inadvertent error, will be happy to make the necessary correction in future printings.

AVON BOOKS
A division of
The Hearst Corporation
105 Madison Avenue
New York, New York 10016

First Avon Books Printing: July 1990

AVON TRADEMARK REG. U.S. PAT. OFF. AND IN OTHER COUNTRIES, MARCA REGISTRADA, HECHO EN U.S.A.

Printed in the U.S.A.

RA 10 9 8 7 6 5 4 3 2 1

Acknowledgments

My thanks to my literary agent, Esther Newberg, for her feisty belief in me; to Susan Kamil, for opening the door into the world of publication; to Hillary Johnson, for listening to my tale over many lunches, while stirring her tea and my mind; to Rachel McCallister, for protecting me from enquiring claws; and to Bob Bender, my gentle and splendid editor.

Thanks to Bonnie Sue Smith and Anne Leffingwell, my West and East Coast typists; and finally, to Grace Ayrsman, who kept my desk and my soul in order.

Contents

Introduction

I started out to write a book called *A Portrait of the Artist as a Housewife*. I wanted to write a collection of stories, poems, and vignettes about things like my toaster oven and my relationships with plumbers, mailmen and delivery people. But life dealt me a much more complicated story. On October 21, 1986, I was diagnosed with ovarian cancer. Suddenly I had to spend all my time getting well. I was fighting for my life against cancer, a more lethal foe than even the interior decorator. The book has turned out a bit differently from what I had intended. It's a book about illness, doctors and hospitals; about friends and family; about beliefs and hopes. It's about my life, especially about the last two years. And I hope it will help others who live in the world of medication and uncertainty.

These are my experiences, of course, and they may not necessarily be what happens to other cancer patients. All the medical explanations in the book are my own, as I understand them. Cancer is probably the most unfunny thing in the world, but I'm a comedienne, and even cancer couldn't stop me from seeing humor in what I went through. So I'm sharing with you what I call a seriously funny book, one that confirms my father's favorite expression about life, "It's always something."

Buddha told a parable in a sutra

A man traveling across a field encountered a
tiger. He fled, the tiger after him. Coming to a
precipice, he caught hold of the root of a wild
vine and swung himself down over the edge. The
tiger sniffed at him from above. Trembling, the
man looked down to where, far below, another
tiger was waiting to eat him. Only the vine
sustained him.
Two mice, one white and one black, little by
little started to gnaw away the vine. The man saw
a luscious strawberry near him. Grasping the
vine with one hand, he plucked the strawberry
with the other.
How sweet it tasted!

Zen Flesh, Zen Bones:
A Collection of Zen and Pre-Zen
Writings, **Compiled by Paul Reps**

1.
The Marriage

Like in the romantic fairy tales I always loved, Gene Wilder and I were married by the mayor of a small village in the south of France, September 18, 1984. We had met in August of 1981, while making the movie *Hanky Panky*, a not-too-successful romantic adventure–comedy –thriller. I had been a fan of Gene Wilder's for many years, but the first time I saw him in person, my heart fluttered—I was hooked. It felt like my life went from black and white to Technicolor. Gene was funny and athletic and handsome, and he smelled good. I was bitten with love and you can tell it in the movie. The brash and feisty comedienne everyone knew from "Saturday Night Live" turned into this shy, demure ingenue with knocking knees. It wasn't good for my movie career, but it changed my life.

Up to that point, I had been a workaholic. I'd taken one job after another for over ten years. But just looking at Gene made me want to stop . . . made me want to cook . . . made me want to start a garden . . . to have a family and settle down. To complicate things, I was married at the time and Gene had been married and divorced twice before and was in no hurry to make another commitment. I lived in a house I had just bought in Connecticut and he lived in Los Angeles. I got an amicable divorce six months later and Gene and I lived together on and off for the next two-and-a-half years. My new "career" became getting him to marry me. I turned down job offers so I could keep myself geographically available. More often than not, I had on a white, frilly apron like Katharine Hepburn in *Woman of the Year* when she left her job to exclusively be Spencer Tracey's wife. Unfortunately, my performing ego wasn't completely content in an apron, and in every screenplay Gene was writing, or project he had under development, I finagled my way into a part.

We were married in the south of France because Gene loved France. If he could have been born French, he would have been—that was his dream.

The only time I had been to France was when I was eighteen. I went with a girlfriend in the sixties when it was popular to go for less than five dollars a day—of course, your parents still gave you a credit card in case you got in trouble. We went on an Icelandic Airlines flight. The plane was so crowded, it seemed like there were twelve seats across and it tilted to whatever side the stewardess was serving on.

We landed in Luxembourg and then our next stop was

Brussels. My girlfriend was of Polish descent, but had been born in Argentina—she spoke four languages fluently. After four days, she was sick of me saying, "What?," "What did they say?"—she couldn't stand me. She just wanted to kill me. I was miserable all through the trip. I was miserable in Luxembourg. I was miserable in Brussels. We slept at the University of Brussels; you could stay there for a dollar a night in the student dormitory, where we spent the evening watching the movie *Greener Pastures* with French subtitles. We went on to Amsterdam where we stayed in a youth hostel. I'll never forget that there was pubic hair on the soap in the bathroom and it made me sick. Years later, I had Roseanne Roseannadanna talk about it.

There I was, eighteen years old in Europe, and all the terrible things that happen to tourists happened to me. In Amsterdam I lost my traveler's checks and spent one whole day looking for the American Express office. I was so upset by the Anne Frank House that I got horrible diarrhea in the lobby of the Rembrandt Museum and never saw one painting. When we went on to France, my girlfriend's boyfriend met us in Paris—romantic Paris! I found the city hectic and weird. Plus, I was on my own. My friend was with her boyfriend; I was the third person —the girl alone.

I don't know why, but everywhere I went, everywhere I looked, a man would be playing with himself. I always have been a starer—a voyeur. I must have been staring too much at other people because I would always get in trouble. I'd be waiting to sit down in a restaurant and a man would come out of the restroom (this must have happened about four or five times), and he would suddenly start staring at me and undoing his fly and playing with himself. Yuck! This wasn't the romantic Paris I had heard of.

I was very isolated because of the language barrier. I felt lonelier than I had ever been. One night after a terrible less-than-two-dollar dinner, I actually ended up running out into the middle of the Champs Elysées trying to get hit by traffic. Yeah, I ran out onto the boulevard and lay down on the ground before the cars came whipping around the corner—you wouldn't believe how fast they come around there. My girlfriend's boyfriend ran out and dragged me back. I was lying down in the street waiting to get run over because I was so lonely and he picked me up and dragged me back. The next day I made a reservation on Air France first class to go home. I only stayed two weeks and spent a fortune flying home. I never went back until Gene took me in 1982. It was the first summer we were living together, and Gene couldn't wait to show me Paris and the French countryside and the southern provinces of the country he adored.

Gene reintroduced Europe to me; and with him I learned it could be a pleasure and I could love it. He took me to one particular château in the mountains in the south of France. We stayed two weeks and I discovered that traveling can be wonderful if you stop to enjoy where you are. Our room was luxurious, with a spectacular view of the Riviera. There was a tennis court and a pool and a restaurant that had one star in the Michelin guidebook. Food was served like precious gems, and I remember we watched the French Open tennis tournament on television in our splendid room, in French. Mats Wilander won.

Tennis is another joy of Gene's life, so I took lessons in California for thirty-five dollars an hour twice a week. I bought a Prince racket and some perky Chris Evert—type outfits, and learned to hit the ball. Gene was infinitely patient with me, hitting balls to me while I klutzed all over the court. I wanted to be M-A-R-R-I-E-D to Gene, but it sure wasn't my tennis game that got him.

Being interested in sports was one of the things Gene wanted in a woman. In the years I lived alone, I loved having sports on television in the background because it made me feel that there were men in the house, but I never sat down and watched it. It was a crazy thing to do, but it just felt safe. With Gene, I became a basketball fan —L.A. Lakers of course, when it was Kareem and Magic, Norm Nixon and Jamaal Wilkes. It looked like ballet to me—stunning and rhythmic. I got hooked not only on watching but on reading about it. Sportswriting is fascinating—descriptions of the opponents and the details of an event in which someone is going to win and someone is going to lose. Life is much longer and more complicated, and the outcomes are less clear-cut.

Not long after our trip to France, we broke up. Gene said he was suffocating, that my needs were smothering him. I was heartsick and back in Connecticut, filled with love and with nowhere to put it. I decided to get a dog. I love dogs, but "Saturday Night Live" and New York City and my career weren't conducive to having pets. My cousins in Detroit used to raise and show Yorkshire terriers so I made a desperate call to them to help me find a dog that was female and already housebroken and small enough that I could travel with her. They found *Sparkle*. Glorious Sparkle with her coal-dark eyes and gray-blond hair, and her nose like a tiny black button.

On Thanksgiving weekend 1982, Sparkle was flown into New York from Michigan, just like me. A young girl who was coming back to college and was a friend of my cousins brought her to New York, right to the hotel where Gene and I were staying to see if we could work out our differences. So Gene and I met Sparkle for the first time together. Then Gene went back to his home in California and I went to my house in Connecticut with Sparkle, where I became one of those people who show you endless pictures of their dog, and all the pictures look alike. I think dogs are the most amazing creatures; they give unconditional love. For me they are the role model for being alive.

Sparkle is a perfect life-form, so little, only five pounds. I designed her haircut 'cause I don't like the way Yorkies look ordinarily, so I have her clipped very short on her body and her head is cut square like a little bear with Dumbo ears. I put various bows and barrettes in her hair to keep it out of her eyes, and she always seems pleased with the process.

I have taken her on television with me when I have been afraid to go alone . . . she's been on the David Letterman show where she did a Stupid Pet Trick. She took a bow on command. She did it on camera perfectly right the first time and they did an instant replay of it. Sparkle goes through things with me. She loves me no matter what I do. She has such a huge personality that if she is not in the house—like if Gene takes her to work with him and I am home—you can feel that she is not there.

Her daily job is guarding me and making sure she gets her two meals a day. I once saw her chase two deer that were nibbling the tops off tulips in my backyard in Connecticut. She bounded across the lawn with her paws barely touching the ground. The deer took off into the woods, but one stopped suddenly and looked back with disdain at this tiny ferocious animal with pink barrettes in its hair.

Gene and I were split up for about five weeks and when we got back together it was under new conditions because there was Sparkle—it wasn't just me, it was me and Sparkle.

In June of 1983 we went back to the south of France and took Sparkle with us. The French people love dogs. They went crazy for ours. She opened doors; she opened their faces and their personalities. Sparkle was allowed to go everywhere with us. She ate in the restaurants sitting on her own chair. She got a real chance to go out and see other people, and she was treated like a queen. I called it the dog's holiday.

In the fall of 1983, Gene and I made our second movie together, *The Woman in Red*. It was a remake of a French film. There really wasn't a part in it for me, but I begged and whined and slept with the writer and the director and the star (all of whom were Gene), and I got a cameo part that turned out to be my first successful movie role. We shot in San Francisco and Los Angeles. At the same time I did promotion for a comedy book I wrote with Alan Zweibel—*Roseanne Roseannadanna's "Hey, Get Back to Work!" Book*. I still had plenty of time to get dinner on the table and involve Gene in endless conversations about commitment and meaningful relationships and child-rearing and meaningful relationships and commitment. He was still fighting for independence and I was all for smothering suffocation.

With the movie in the can, Gene and Sparkle and I were on our way for our holiday in France again. We were taking an early morning flight from Los Angeles to New York so we could visit Gene's sister and brother-in-law on the way. Because we had the dog, they put us in a private passenger lounge to wait for the flight. I put Sparkle down on the floor and she was running around being cute when I saw her sniffing something in a corner. When I knelt down, there were these little turquoise pellets spilling out of a box on the floor. The box clearly said, "RAT POISON." There was a woman from the travel agency with us. I gasped—I didn't know if Sparkle had eaten a pellet or not. Gene said, "She wouldn't eat that," but I was frightened. What if she had eaten one? I wanted to stick my finger down the dog's throat.

We called the poison center and gave them the number on the box and the name of the poison. "'Get her to a vet immediately," said the voice on the other end. I just picked up Sparkle, said to Gene, "I am going to the vet, I will meet you in New York later," kissed him goodbye and ran out. My luggage was already on the plane, which was scheduled to leave in twenty minutes. The woman from the travel agency went with me. We flagged down a limo that was just dropping somebody off. I was panicked now—the hysterical mother—screaming, "Get us to the nearest vet!" I knew I had seen some on the way to the airport. We found Airport Cities Animal Hospital in Inglewood, and rushed the dog in. The vet was just getting to work and putting on his coat when I ran in yelling, "My dog ate rat poison!" I was white as a ghost and Sparkle was just wagging her tail—la-la-la. He was a wonderful vet; we gave him the information, he called the poison center and they told him what to do. He gave Sparkle an injection that caused her to throw up a turquoise pellet —she *had* eaten one. This pellet contained rat poison that kills the rat by causing its blood not to coagulate. The rat bleeds to death eventually but it gets very thirsty first. That way it won't die in the airport where people are, but will go away to find water and die a slow, horrible death away from the building. If I hadn't spotted that box, Sparkle would have gradually gotten ill and we wouldn't have known why.

In the meantime, Gene's plane went out on the runway, had mechanical difficulty and had to come back. Because I was with the travel agent, she had called the agency and told them where we were. They let Gene get off the plane to come and call me so I was able to tell him that Sparkle did eat the poison and he knew I had done the right thing. He went on to New York where his sister and brother-in-law were waiting, and I stayed the whole day in the vet's office holding Sparkle. The injection made her anxious and she trembled all day. She had to go on a program of vitamin K injections for two weeks, which kept the blood coagulating in case any pellet had dissolved and gone into her system. The vet let me be the nurse and take her home. I still had to take her back every day for the injections, so when Gene got to New York I spoke to him and said:

"You go on to France. You need the holiday and there is nothing you can do here. I'll take care of Sparkle now and when you get back everything will be fine."

Gene did go, but he went thinking, *Well, she has definitely grown up, she has matured.* I wouldn't let him out of my sight before then, and this was me acting in a very responsible way.

When Gene came back from France, he gave me an engagement ring. Our cousin Buddy now refers to it as the time when Sparkle tried to commit suicide because Gene wasn't marrying Gilda. He believes that Sparkle's "suicide attempt" was what turned Gene around and made him actually ask me to get married. So you can see why I owed a great deal to that dog.

After a successful summer release in the U.S., *The Woman in Red* opened in Europe in the fall of 1984. The movie company sent Gene and me on a publicity tour in Europe. (Of course Sparkle came too.) And between the Deauville Film Festival and interviews in Rome, we stopped in the south of France and got married.

We had to climb up the cobblestoned streets of the thirteenth-century village to get to the mayor's office. The whole ceremony was in French and I didn't understand a word. I would wait till there was a pause and then say, *"Oui"* (I do). Then, the mayor would have to say, *"Attendez! Attendez!"* (Wait! Wait!), so I'd wait for the next pause. For a comedienne, my timing was really off. I was ahead of the whole thing. It was raining that day and someone said that meant good luck, but I have a feeling people say things like that so you won't feel so bad wearing a raincoat over your wedding gown.

I created my own bridal outfit. I wore a straw hat with my hair piled on top of my head under it, and stuck flowers in the ribbon on the black brim. I wore culottes

—long gray culottes and black tights and black ballet shoes. I wore gray because this was my second marriage, but on top I wore a white silk blouse with lace on the collar and sleeves. Gene wore a dark blue sport jacket and beige pants. He bought a new striped wedding tie in the village and carried an umbrella. Sparkle was there. I called her "the bridesdog" and she wore a small straw hat too, with pink streamers. I held her in my arms with a traditional French wedding bouquet.

Our wedding party consisted of Gene's sister and her husband and some friends of ours who own a Danish restaurant in the south of France and a Belgian couple who are our close friends from Los Angeles. The manager of the château where we were staying and her assistant were our witnesses because they were permanent residents of the town. There was one photographer there. He snapped a photo that was on the cover the next day of *Nice Matin,* the local newspaper. It was Gene and I under the umbrella holding the dog in the middle of the old village with the cobblestones all around us, and behind us there was a woman peeking around the corner, breast-feeding a baby, and a big black dog watching—just so naturally—to see what all the commotion was about. That was on the cover of all the papers with a two-page article that I could never read because it was in French.

As Americans, you can't just get married in France. There is a lot of legal rigmarole that has to be accomplished. For instance, our birth certificates and marriage documents and divorce papers all had to be translated into French and sent on to the mayor's office. We also had to have specific blood tests taken by a doctor in New York who was officially approved by the French government.

We found his office in the basement of a building in the West Fifties. There was no receptionist and the doctor greeted us in his shirtsleeves. He filled in our application on an old portable Olivetti typewriter and asked for his payment in cash. Gene paid and the doctor put the money in his pocket. Either he didn't recognize us or he wasn't a fan, because he never indicated that this was more than routine or—at best—a bit of an annoyance.

I went into the examining room to have my blood taken first, probably because I wanted to get it over with fast. The equipment seemed to be from the 1920s. Everything looked too small and a bit rusty. The doctor said he needed a urine specimen, but instead of giving me a plastic cup, he told me to pee in this big porcelain dish and leave it on the bathroom floor like a dog's bowl. Without speaking, he weighed me, and took my pulse and blood pressure. I sat nervously on the examining table with my one sleeve rolled up. He unwrapped a syringe and stuck the needle into a vein in my arm to get blood. No blood came up into the needle. For a minute I thought maybe there was no blood in me, but the doctor muttered something about the needle being defective and stuck me again—no blood. He yanked the needle out and walked back over to the glass jar with the rusty metal lid to get another syringe.

I screamed for Gene to come into the room. This was a nightmare. Gene came right in and I said: "Gene, why don't you go first, there's no blood coming out of me." The doctor muttered again about a defective needle.

Gene said, "What are you scared of?"

I said, "Nothing—I'm not scared! You go ahead, you go first, I have to go for a walk."

I was going to leave. I was not going to get married because I couldn't handle this guy jabbing me with needles. I went out on the street and tried to call my psychiatrist from a phone booth, but the line was busy. I thought, *Should I go through with this? Should I let this doctor take my blood and maybe infect me with some horrible disease with his defective needle?* It had taken me three years to get Gene to marry me and now this sleazy little doctor was going to ruin it.

When I went back in, Gene and the doctor were chatting about France. With Gene, the blood had come right out. I made Gene stay in the room and hold my hand while I let the doctor stick me again. He got the blood this time. So we'd be able to get married after all. The next day, my arm turned black and blue all up and down the inside and it stayed that way for weeks.

After the mayor completed our wedding ceremony, we all rode in three cars to another small village and climbed the mountain to the restaurant of our Danish friends. They served smoked salmon hors d'oeuvres and opened bottles of champagne and everyone toasted our marriage. Later in the evening at the château dining room, we had a traditional French wedding dinner. Gene had hired two musicians to come and play for us so we could dance— a guitarist and a violinist. The violinist was actually a government official—the assistant to the mayor of Nice— but he loved playing at private parties. They followed us everywhere with music, accompanying our moods—it reminded me of a French comedy.

It was without a doubt a brilliant way of getting married. A perfect wedding day; symbolically, the three couples who were able to come all had working marriages based on love. We invited everyone who was eating in the dining room to have some of our wedding cake and to get up and dance and celebrate with us. For something old, Gene's sister gave me a bracelet that had belonged to their mother. I borrowed every bobby pin she had to hold my hat on that evening. I wore a dress I had bought in Paris just that week for something new, and someone sent me a lace garter from Los Angeles and Sparkle wore it around her neck—it was blue.

The French are not noted for their comediennes. It is rare that you hear of a French woman in comedy. They called me *"Charlot"* in the subsequent articles about our marriage: "Gene Wilder Marries a *Charlot*"—their word for "Charlie Chaplin." When the journalists asked Gene, "Why didn't you marry the beautiful girl in *The Woman in Red?*" he would always reply, "I did!"

We really had our honeymoon in Rome between press conferences and interviews. Like I said, it was all very romantic. I loved Rome and so did Sparkle. She went everywhere in my purse with just her head sticking out. She was so quiet and well-behaved that she slipped by the guards and saw Michelangelo's *Moses.* We spent hours traipsing through the Vatican. When we got to the Sistine Chapel, she was very busy smelling the crowds of people, but I made sure she looked up at the ceiling.

Gene flew on to London and Copenhagen to do more publicity for the movie, and I flew home to Connecticut because Sparkle couldn't go into those countries without going into quarantine. It was a nine-hour flight from

Rome to New York. We ate four times and Sparkle stayed in her doggie travel case underneath the seat in front of me during the meal service. The rest of the flight she snuggled beside me in the seat and ate snacks. Ten days later Gene flew home to us in Connecticut, and we began our married life.

The mayor had given me a French family book along with our marriage certificate. It was funny—it was all in French, but it had our names in it: Gilda Radner from Detroit, Michigan, and Gene Wilder from Milwaukee, Wisconsin. We were supposed to write in the names of our children as they came.

When I got home, I ordered stationery that said "Gilda Wilder" and "Mr. and Mrs. G. Wilder." I was uneasy for a while trying to figure out when to be Gilda Radner, the TV star, when to be Gilda Wilder, a brand-new person, when to be Mrs. Gene Wilder, the wife of the international movie star, and when to be Mrs. G. Wilder, just another blushing bride.

I decided I could be them all.

2.

The Baby and the Movie Star

After being Mrs. Wilder for a week, I drove into New York City from Connecticut to see a radiologist whom my gynecologist had recommended. I had to have a hysterosalpingogram. This is an X-ray technique that involves injecting a radiopaque dye in the uterus. The dye outlines the cavity of the uterus and the fallopian tubes to show whether the tubes are open or blocked.

For almost a year before my marriage I had stopped using any form of birth control. I figured my pregnancy was another surefire way to get Gene . . . but pregnancy hadn't come.

I saw the dye running through my reproductive system on a closed-circuit screen in the examining room. There I was lying on a table with my legs spread apart watching the worst show I'd ever seen on television. The show was called "My Tubes Were Closed." It was about a thirty-eight-year-old newlywed who finds out she's infertile. Those tubes have to be open for an egg to get fertilized and slide into the uterus. I remember the attending nurse looking at the screen with a long, sad face and me asking, "What's wrong?" and her saying:

"Your gynecologist will explain it to you—we really can't give you all the information."

Then her face dropped even longer. I mean, what could be lovelier than Gilda Radner and Gene Wilder having a baby? The hair alone would make people squeal with delight. But my tubes were definitely closed.

My gynecologist told me that there were a couple of routes that I could take. One was in vitro fertilization—a procedure in which an egg is removed from a ripe follicle in an ovary and fertilized by a sperm cell outside the human body, then reinserted into the uterus. The other was that I could have major surgery to open the tubes. Or we could adopt.

Gene and I talked about our options. We both wanted a family, but Gene made it clear to me that our relationship was the most important thing to him—that a baby was best off coming into the world to two people who were happy together. He said most of the decision was mine, but he was willing to help me and to do whatever we needed to do, but not to do anything that would jeopardize our marriage. I saw motherhood as the next logical step in my life; I refused to accept the infertility sentence that was handed out to me.

I found it very difficult to literally make the decision to have a baby. When it comes to you, when it just happens easily, it is still the biggest gamble in the world. It is the glorious life force ... what's meant to be—but really to create a human being is a huge thing. It's huge and scary —it's an act of infinite optimism. Suddenly, when it's not going to be a natural event and it's put into your hands with experimental procedures and elective surgeries, the decision becomes an obsession. For me the issue became less whether I wanted a baby or not and more my inability to accept not being able to have one.

I had been pregnant in the sixties, and at nineteen years old had had an illegal abortion that probably influenced the messy state of my reproductive organs. For the next nineteen years my priority was to finish my education and pursue my career. Now I couldn't take my fate: You'll never have a baby. That was the sentence handed to me. I began to beat my fists against a door that maybe I had locked on the other side.

Gene and I flew back to California in October of 1984. He was already working on a new screenplay called *Haunted Honeymoon*. It took place in America in 1934 and was about a radio performer whose family tries to scare him to death. It was supposed to be a "comedy chiller." Gene was to be the radio performer and I wanted to be (what else?) his wife. Gene worked every day at his office. Meanwhile I started a screenplay with a friend. You cannot live in Los Angeles for any period of time without eventually trying to write a screenplay. It's like a flu bug that you catch ... even the plumber has a screenplay in his truck.

In the meantime, I found out everything about the in vitro fertilization program at UCLA. I found a doctor who would let me into the program. In simple terms, it begins with a surgical procedure called a laparoscopy—that's where the doctors look at the condition and placement of your reproductive organs by putting an instrument through an incision in your belly button. It is an outpatient procedure, but it is a minor surgery that requires general anesthesia. If everything checks out, you can proceed with the program.

What happens next, in even simpler terms, is that certain hormones are injected into you daily that make your ovaries release more eggs than usual. The doctors watch your ovaries through ultrasound readings, and when you have matured enough eggs they put you under general anesthesia again to aspirate, or remove, the eggs. They are then mixed with your husband's sperm in a dish or test tube after which the fertilized eggs are put back inside you in a procedure much like a regular gynecological exam. This is followed by more hormone injections daily to ensure that these eggs will implant onto the uterine wall. The process has to be done at a certain time in your menstrual cycle and the whole thing can stop at any time if something goes wrong—like your ovaries don't respond properly to the hormones, or whatever.

The in vitro team at UCLA were very excited about their results. I got caught up in their enthusiasm and convinced Gene to do the same.

During the procedure, the woman can go to the hospital to get her daily hormone injections, but the doctors prefer that the husband give the shots so that he can feel more involved. Gene had been in the medical corps in the army and had given shots before, but I still made him practice on an orange and a grapefruit about a hundred times. He gave me my first injection in an examining room at UCLA with a nurse and doctor in the room. He was great. From then on, Gene gave me two shots a day at home.

As we moved toward conception, foreplay for me consisted of filling myself with liquids every morning to make my bladder large enough to move it out of the way for the ultrasound picture to show my ovaries. Then I'd drive over mountains and bumpy roads to UCLA to sit on my leg in a waiting room filled with women who all had to pee so desperately that they would rip each other's eyes out to have their ultrasound first.

On the day my ultrasound showed I had matured enough eggs, Gene's foreplay began. That evening, he gave me an injection to induce ovulation and the next morning he drove me to the hospital for my second laparoscopy. While they wheeled me into surgery to aspirate the eggs, they put Gene in a little utility room by himself. He was right next door to the laboratory where a technician would wash his sperm and join it in a test tube with my surgically removed eggs. He described the room to me later. There was a washbasin with a wooden shelf above it that held a small plastic container and a piece of paper with instructions for keeping the sperm sterile. There was no chair or window in the room, but there were a mop and a bucket and a stack of *Playboy* and *Penthouse* magazines with a note that said, "If you require help," Gene said the instructions were rather vague about when to wash and how to dry your hands. He said the pressure was overwhelming—him sitting on the floor with his pants around his ankles in the gray cement room. He was supposed to knock on the door when he had the sperm. He told me he thought he was going to go crazy. It wasn't exactly romantic. He kept thinking, *My wife's going to have surgery and what if I can't do this?*

Miraculously, everything worked. My ovaries matured eight eggs, and Gene knocked on the door. Seven of the eggs fertilized in the dish. The happy Wilders went home and returned the next day to have four of the fertilized eggs put into my uterus. We had to sign a paper allowing them to throw three of the fertilized eggs away. They didn't have freezing equipment at UCLA at the time, and there was too great a risk of multiple births and danger to the mother if seven or more eggs were returned to the uterus.

On the morning that was to be the moment of conception, I was lying on the examining table while Gene sat close to my head and held my hand. As I looked between my legs, I could see my three doctors—one a sandy-haired Protestant, the other a young Chinese-American, and the third a dark-skinned Sephardic Jew. The room was quiet and the lights were dim as the Protestant doctor placed the fertilized eggs into my uterus, the other two watching intently. I was reminded of the World War II memorial statue where all the different nationalities are putting the American flag in the ground at Iwo Jima.

I spent the next six hours in a dark hospital room. I wasn't allowed to read or watch TV or talk to anyone. I was to stay calm and lie with the bed tilted at a certain angle. This was to help ensure that the eggs would attach to the uterine wall. I got very anxious and very hungry, and they ended up having to give me a tranquilizer and two slices of whole-wheat toast.

For nineteen days after that, Gene had to keep giving me progesterone shots. That is the hormone you produce naturally in your body before you get your period. It made me irritable and moody. I was told to stay at home and do quiet activities, but a week later I started to bleed. The doctors told me to lie down, but I wasn't just spotting. To me it looked like someone shot a deer. I bled heavily for a few days and then continued to spot. They wouldn't let me quit taking the progesterone—I knew that I was miscarrying but they wouldn't let me quit because this was an experimental procedure and they had to follow their protocol. They made me keep taking the progesterone the whole nineteen days because they said a woman could bleed and still be pregnant. On the twentieth day, they did a blood test and it was negative—there was no pregnancy.

As horrible as it was, I would have repeated the procedure, but Gene said to me, "I will never do that again." I couldn't do it without Gene. But at this point, I'd lost interest in everything else. I was desperate not to *not* have a baby.

I cried right through Christmas and into 1985. By February I had booked myself for major surgery to have my tubes opened. This is a serious operation—it can involve six to eight hours of microsurgery, but I was determined. Gene could only say, "If that's what you want." I had the operation and I completely recuperated in a week's time.

My tubes were open and I was elated. All we had to do now was to have sex at just the right time of the month —at exactly the moment I was ovulating. Well, I'll tell you, that was the worst pressure in the world. It was as consuming as the in vitro program and I drove Gene nuts. It was the kind of obsession they show in the movies, made worse by my age. I was thirty-eight years old and my biological time clock was breaking the sound barrier.

I bought one of those new ovulation kits where you are the scientist. You have to catch your first urine of the morning in a cup, mix it with some powder, wait ten minutes, mix something else, wait ten minutes, mix it with another thing, wait a half hour, dip a stick into the mixture and match it up with a color chart to see whether it is blue or green or yellow. The kit costs about eighty dollars for one cycle. I didn't tell Gene I was doing this. He was already wondering about my sanity.

One morning I couldn't unscrew the lid with the mixing stuff in it. I was going crazy because if you don't do it in exactly ten minutes, the whole test is ruined. So I had to run into the bedroom where Gene was still asleep. I poked him and said, "Don't ask me any questions, just take the lid off this vial." He did it and never asked me about it. He was sound asleep.

I ran back to my room and started mixing. My color chart was all set up under an appropriate light. I mixed, then waited a half hour—the dipstick in the liquid turned blue. The blue matched the blue on the chart, which meant I was ovulating. I ran back into the bedroom and calmly woke Gene and told him that we had to have sex right that second. I never let on about this expensive ovulation kit.

My ovaries became the center of my universe. Everything, even my brain, was down there all the time. I thought if I really concentrated, I would be able to tell when I was ovulating—I could feel what was happening there. I would be so relieved a few days after my period when it wasn't a time for fertility, so I could relax, but then as soon as I got to the middle of the cycle, the panic came in. I was always counting days on my calendar. Then when I got my period; it was like a death—a failure —another lost child.

Orion Pictures gave Gene the okay on *Haunted Honeymoon*. It was a "go" picture in April of 1985, to be shot in England, directed by Gene Wilder and starring Gene Wilder, Gilda Radner and Dom DeLuise. I swear Gene is the only person I have ever slept with to get a part in a movie. It is never easy to get a movie made, but *Woman in Red* was a nice enough success to make the movie company confident in sending us out again. Because the English pound was much weaker at the time than the American dollar, the exchange rate made it possible to shoot the movie in England for nine million dollars when it would have cost over thirteen million in the U.S.

The idea of working and living in London over the next year delighted Gene. I began a slow, desperate internal panic. Sparkle could not go to England. England has strict quarantine rules because it is an island. No yacht on the Thames, no helicopter drop-off, no underground smuggling ring could help. Sparkle could not go to England without spending six months in quarantine. Now you might be saying to yourself that, after all, this was just a dog—but not to me. Sparkle was my baby. I felt very torn about leaving her even for the three months that I was required to be in London for the movie. Gene and I decided not to stay in London for the six months of pre-production and the casting of the movie; instead, Gene would make several trips back and forth and I would stay with Sparkle in America. For one month I'd take Sparkle to the south of France and Gene would visit us there. This was our way of making the movie and staying with Sparkle.

I continued to dwell on the fact that every time Gene traveled and we weren't together, I was missing an ovulation cycle—an opportunity to have a child. What I created was a tremendously stressful time in my life. I wanted to have everything—I wanted to be the costar of the movie; I wanted to be with Gene all the time; I wanted to have a baby; and I wanted to have the dog with me. I knew that traveling all over the place wasn't so good for my menstrual cycle. I knew that I needed to be with Gene, but the dog couldn't go, and the dog was my little baby. I had to leave the baby that already existed to pursue the baby that might be. I put myself into a terrible, stressful panic. I made it all so important that I thought my brain would pop.

In June, we flew to Connecticut where I stayed and prepared for my part in the movie while Gene went to London to cast the picture and find a place for us to live. When Gene returned three weeks later, both of us began to question the timing of our sexual activity. We thought that maybe we should abstain from having a baby now because a movie company was spending a lot of money on us. I couldn't play my part in the picture if I became pregnant. So suddenly we faced a new dilemma—do we want the movie or the baby? We decided to use birth control. It seemed weird that after in vitro fertilization and tubal surgery and eighty-dollar ovulation kits, I, the perpetrator, was choosing to put off having a baby in order to be a movie star. But my career was still very important to me, too.

Then came the day when I had to send Sparkle back to California where Gene's secretary was going to take care of her for three months. I acted it out like a major tragedy. A friend of mine was flying back to California and took Sparkle with her. I went to the airport. I held Sparkle in my arms until the flight attendant insisted that everyone board the plane. Then I broke into such a gush of tears that Sparkle's head got wet. They boarded the 747 bound for L.A.—my friend, my dog and the official airline pet traveling case. I stood weeping until I saw the plane safely take off. Sparkle never even looked back.

England turned out to be gorgeous in the fall. We had a house there—narrow and five flights tall. It was in the area called Belgravia near Victoria Station—quaint and wonderful streets lined with little shops and pubs and townhouse gardens. I had to go to work immediately, fitting costumes, deciding on styles for my hair, thinking about the period of the movie—the 1930s—and how my nails would be, what hats and accessories would be appropriate. I began meeting a whole new group of people, all of whom would be helping me to be wonderful in *Haunted Honeymoon.*

I was determined to be a movie star. My mind conjured up images of Ginger Rogers and Carole Lombard—beautiful women so large on the screen, taking people out of their lives and into specially lit fantasies. Television was earthbound, but the movies were up in the stars.

They were trying different makeups on me, giving me screen tests, elaborate costumes—everything. Hats were tilted in different directions on my head and warm lights were adjusted to make me look my best. I had been in movies before, but there was something especially glamorous about this one. I was the leading lady, so everything had to be just right.

When Gene makes a movie, the people who work on it have such a love for him that the set is always a happy place. The cast and crew were mostly English except for Dom DeLuise and me and Gene and our dear friend the actress Julann Griffin. Dom and his wife, Carol, came to London but were not there the entire shoot because of previous commitments Dom had in the United States. Julann and I spent every day off together shopping and exploring London.

We began shooting the first day of September in 1985. On September 18, I was sitting—in my folding canvas movie-star chair wearing this luscious black-and-white evening gown—when the assistant director called me to go onto the shooting stage in the next room. At the same time, Gene was called onto the set from his trailer wearing his blue-and-white-striped pajamas. As the two of us appeared on opposite sides of the room, the cast and crew, who had gathered in a group, began singing "For He's a Jolly Good Fellow" at the top of their lungs. A huge cake sparkled in the light of one candle. It was our wedding anniversary—our first-year wedding anniversary and here we were on a movie set with the whole cast and crew around us. Just like our wedding day, it was a perfect time. We were thinking what wonderful lives we had—that we could be married in the south of France and have our first wedding anniversary in London, England. The cameramen filmed the event.

Over the next few weeks I got heavily into the adventure of moviemaking—up before the sun and asleep by nine at night. A driver took me to and from the set, and on any errands I needed to go on. Gene had his own driver because we were often on separate schedules. When the weekends came, we were exhausted. But Saturdays I did the laundry and shopped for Sunday dinner. The English shops close by one o'clock on Saturdays so supplies had to be gathered quickly. We always played tennis on Saturday afternoons at different private courts and ate a big Italian meal on Saturday nights at a restaurant called Mimmo's around the corner from our flat. Sometimes on Saturday nights, if we weren't too tired, we found time to make love. Sundays we played tennis or went to a movie, but I always cooked salmon steaks and baked potatoes and broccoli with delicious English whole-grain bread and fruit and shortbread cookies for dessert. Gene was always working on his next day's shooting schedule and I did my vocal and dance exercises. Except when I was complaining about something I did or didn't do in the movie, life fell into a pleasant pattern. The weather stayed miraculously warm and I loved being a pampered movie star and an English housewife.

The shooting of *Haunted Honeymoon* required me to wear a wedding gown almost every day for two months. I looked like a bride all the time and people seemed to treat me that way too. My makeup woman did my makeup at about six-thirty every morning. I would always joke with her about how my face was going to break out before my period and she would have her work cut out for her. But my skin was looking very good and I didn't even think to look at my calendar until I got the first dizzy spell. My calendar showed that my period was late.

I couldn't believe it. It had been the last thing on my mind.

I sent my dresser, Jenny, out to get me one of those home pregnancy tests that show results in an hour. If your urine made a bull's-eye appear in this tube, you were pregnant. Bull's-eye! I made Jenny run out and buy two more kits. She said they were already congratulating her at the chemist's where she bought them. Bull's-eye again! The last kit (a different kind) I took home so Gene could do the test. A stick had to turn blue. It did.

We were shocked. We walked around Belgravia, our English neighborhood. Gene had the blue stick in his pocket. The weather was warm and we held on to each other and sang quietly while our brains darted through this new phase of our life. We like to sing the song "Ohio" in harmony whenever we are happy, mainly because I've got the harmony down for the whole song except for one line near the end. I never get it right and that always makes us laugh. People say pregnancy never happens when you really want it to; it comes at the wrong time. This was absolutely the wrong time. I hadn't been thinking about it. Neither of us had. I hadn't been straining and struggling, but that is when they say it happens —when you aren't thinking about it.

I went to a doctor and had the pregnancy confirmed with a blood test. He said, "Go ahead and live your life however you would—having a baby is the most natural thing in the world." The next few days I was filled with emotion. I got a little irritable and I remember I cried on the set one day. I had a fight with someone, which I never would do, and a depression set in. I didn't worry because

I'd heard many people say the first three months of their pregnancies they were really irritable because of hormonal changes. I didn't have any nausea, but I was very tired and high-strung. I felt swollen up—my breasts were getting really big and they ached.

One morning a week later, I woke up and felt relieved. It was like someone had drained the water out of me. I went to the bathroom and I was bleeding—bleeding heavily. I was having another miscarriage. It was so soon, only a week after the pregnancy had been confirmed. Gene was already at work. I phoned the doctor and he said I could go lie down, but I would have to stay that way for weeks and weeks. I knew I had to be on the set in a few hours. They were shooting a banquet scene—I would just have to sit at a table all day. I decided to go to work and try to stay calm. The bleeding continued. I told Gene privately in his trailer—and together we made the choice for me to stay at work. We mourned quietly. We were glad we hadn't told too many people. We were creating a movie. *Haunted Honeymoon* was a third of the way "in the can." I bled for two weeks. I went to the doctor and had an ultrasound to make sure the miscarriage was complete.

I really didn't cry as much as I thought I would. It wasn't the usual great explosion of disappointment. I became very philosophical about the whole thing. I had the movie—I would now be able to do the big flying scene in the harness that I'd rehearsed. Gene was wonderful about it. What could we do? We accepted that this wasn't the right time for me to be pregnant. There would be other times. Gene was more frightened that I would have a breakdown, which I didn't seem to have. I thought it just wasn't meant to be, and besides, people had said that they had had miscarriages first and then pregnancies right after. At least I knew it was possible for me to get pregnant. I was so busy making the movie every day and loving it—being the coddled baby a movie star can be —that I threw myself into my work.

3.

Forty

I bounced back quickly from the miscarriage, but not too long afterward I caught a cold that was going around. The studio could get very damp and chilly and the cold settled in my respiratory system and wouldn't go away. I never felt one hundred percent well after that. They say that you aren't aware of your health until you lose it. It's something I'd always just taken for granted. I had always had energy—too much energy. I was the type of person who had to say, "It's three o'clock—I'd better run around the block or I won't be able to sleep tonight," or "I'd better go swim forty lengths or I'll be tossing and turning." The last couple of weeks in England I just didn't have any energy. I slipped on the stairs in our flat and hit the small of my back. That slowed me down for weeks. I'd feel good for a few days and I'd think I was fine and then I'd wake up one day and feel like I was getting the flu. I'd think I had a fever, so from my life's experience with illness I would say, "I'm getting the flu." But then I would never get the flu. I would feel okay the next day and then a week would go by and I would wake up one morning and feel like I was getting something again. I'd drink a whole lot of liquids and take vitamin C and the next day I would be okay again. I didn't have to miss work on the set, but something was definitely wrong.

We finished filming *Haunted Honeymoon* in the middle of November 1985. Then we flew back to Connecticut where I was joyously reunited with Sparkle, who was in perfect health and was plenty mad at me for the first ten days or so. She wouldn't eat or play. She would just stare at me with those "where-the-hell-did-you-go?" eyes. She definitely forgave me on Thanksgiving. I prepared the entire meal, turkey, stuffing, cranberry relish, the works! I was thrilled to be back in America and Sparkle got extra under-the-table handouts.

We were back in Los Angeles by Christmas. I had my hair permed and my eyelashes dyed black. I'd come back to find my screenwriting partner was married and pregnant and working on the staff of a situation comedy. Our screenplay had to be shelved for a while . . . so I busied myself reading scripts and writing little vignettes about my life as a housewife. We were redoing our living room and bathroom in Los Angeles and I was inextricably involved with painters, plumbers, tilers and interior decorators. I also started the world's most expensive course in French in reaction to our wedding ceremony. I still think every sentence I learned cost about ten dollars per word, but I enjoyed playing the lesson tapes in the car and repeating whatever Pierre and Marie said. I also liked the idea of going to school and having coffee and a cigarette in the lounge. Gene and I rang in 1986 with smoked salmon and old movies on TV.

Then on a Sunday, maybe the first Sunday of 1986, Gene and I were in the car on our way to play tennis at a friend's house. Suddenly, my eyelids got very heavy. It was as though I was hypnotized into this deep sleep. I had slept well the night before and I wasn't sick, but a feeling of uncontrollable tiredness came over me . . . like a fog rolling in over my brain that I couldn't escape. I was listless the rest of the day and slept that night and into the next day in that same relentless fog. It was a new element added to my on-and-off flu symptoms. It scared me.

I made an appointment to see my internist immediately. He gave me a total physical. I had all my blood work done and chest X-rays and an electrocardiogram—the whole deal. There was nothing wrong with me. The internist ran a test for something called Epstein-Barr virus. The blood test showed that I had elevated antibodies for Epstein-Barr virus. Every other level of my blood was fine. The internist said he didn't really believe there was such a thing as Epstein-Barr virus, that it was the new fad illness—a catchall disease—like hypoglycemia in the sixties. If it did exist, there was no cure for it. It wasn't life-threatening—it would eventually go away. He thought my symptoms might just be from depression.

This internist had been my doctor for a few years and had listened to various complaints. He knew about my endless baby-quest. I was never a hypochondriac, but I was capable of getting very neurotic over any health disturbance. I hated to be sick and I had an imagination that could turn a stomachache into the plague. After all, endless neurotic babbling about things was often the basis of my comedy, but it also showed up in my doctor's office. I had crowned myself "the Queen of Neurosis." I worried too much. I felt guilty too often. I "what-iffed" every situation. I found my own behavior irritating and endearing at the same time. The internist patted me on the back and told me to stop worrying. "Just relax . . . it'll burn itself out."

In the next couple of weeks I ran a low-grade fever. I called up the internist and said, "I'm running a fever."

He asked, "How high?"

"Not much—very low—ninety-nine, a hundred."

He said, "It's nothing to worry about. Take aspirin or Tylenol to treat the fever—it can happen in this Epstein-Barr virus."

I hung up, but I kept thinking about how he said he didn't really think there was such a thing as Epstein-Barr virus.

So the "weird life" continued. I would be fine maybe for ten days and then seemingly around my menstrual cycle I would go into this severe fatigue and run a low-grade fever, then I would be okay again. I tried to get as much done as possible when I felt well because I knew the fatigue was going to come again. Then just when it started to develop a pattern, it would totally surprise me. For example, I wouldn't be able to get out of bed for two or three days. Gene would have to cancel social engagements or go alone.

I started to become depressed about living with the uncertainty of my health. My appetite remained good and my internist said there was nothing to worry about. He became more convinced that depression was the culprit. I wondered which came first, the illness or the depression. There were enough things to be depressed about —trying to have a baby, the miscarriages, career uncertainties, the prospect of turning forty. On the other hand, I had a wonderful husband, two beautiful homes, had just completed a movie, and was writing and enjoying life in California. The scale of good and bad didn't seem out of balance, or any more tipped than it had ever been.

In March Gene returned to Connecticut in preparation for a month's trip to London where he would do the sound mix on *Haunted Honeymoon*. My plans were to go to London with Gene. We had already booked a suite in a small hotel in our old neighborhood. We were both looking forward to it. Our friend Grace, who is the caretaker of our Connecticut home, agreed to look after Sparkle for the month. Grace is originally from the Midwest, a divorced grandmother who lives with her sister and brother-in-law about a half-mile down the road, or, as she'd say, "down the pike." I consider her a member of the family, and I knew Sparkle would be fine with her.

I came to Connecticut a few days later than Gene because I was offered a screen test for a movie. I had never had to do a screen test before, but there were quite a few actresses under consideration. I liked the movie, but the deal fell apart, and the screen test never happened. When I joined Gene, I was upset and disappointed. I felt my career had slipped out of my control. I had been a big television star, but my movie career hadn't gone well enough for me to call the shots.

The day before our flight, the fog rolled in again, and

I fell into a heavy fatigue. I couldn't get out of bed. Maybe it *was* depression—the career disappointment. Gene took the flight to London alone. All I could do was kiss him goodbye and say I'd join him in a week when I felt better. That week in April 1986, terrorism was on the news every night. I was scared to fly anyway, but this only made it worse. Just the same, I packed my bags and was determined to go. The night before my trip, my travel agent called and said my flight was canceled. I don't remember why but there was so much going on at the airports those days. Perhaps there weren't enough people on that flight to make the trip. Americans stopped flying to Europe. There was fear at all the airports and intense security. Gene and I spoke on the phone every day. We talked about how the whole world felt on edge. The same day my flight was canceled they found the lady in London's Heathrow Airport taking explosives onto an El Al flight. Gene suddenly said, "I don't want you to come. It's too dangerous. I'd worry too much."

My bags remained packed for the next three weeks. Every day I thought I might go. I was glued to the television set, waiting for the next thing to happen. And then it happened—*Chernobyl*. The fear of going abroad increased. There was a nuclear cloud over Europe and my husband was there. America waited to see which way the winds would blow. I stayed home.

During that month of April, I started having weird pelvic cramping. I went to see a gynecologist in Connecticut. He ran a series of blood tests that showed absolutely nothing wrong and he said what I had was mittelschmerz, meaning that during the time of ovulation I could sometimes get severe cramping. He said that many women have even gone to the hospital and had surgery thinking it was something serious, but it was just what he called mittelschmerz. So there I was with this painful reminder that I was ovulating and Gene and I were apart. Now I had Epstein-Barr virus and mittelschmerz: fitting diseases for the Queen of Neurosis. A girlfriend of mine from L.A. told me about a young woman in Washington, D.C., who had greatly helped another friend with health problems through vitamins and nutrition. I called the nutritionist and within a week I was taking megadoses of vitamin C and about forty other pills a day with promises of renewed health and fertility.

Gene returned, and Sparkle and I and fifteen pounds of vitamins went to the south of France for our vacation. It had become an annual trip—to go back to the place where we got married, to spend Gene's birthday there and to have this wonderful vacation life. Despite all of the scares of traveling and anti-American feelings around the world, I knew that I was going to make this trip. I had been away from Gene for so long that I was definitely going to make this trip to France and have a grand time. I went bravely, oddly enough when no other Americans were going to Europe. There I was, the Queen of Neurosis, jumping on a plane, next to my husband, with my dog, calm, easygoing, taking off, landing, marching through customs. Only occasionally did I wonder which passenger had a gun in his bag, or whether we would be blown out of the side of the plane.

We arrived in Paris, ate omelettes for dinner at a little bistro and spent the night. The next morning we flew to the south of France. The three weeks that we spent there were wonderful. The weather was beautiful. I felt relatively good. I knew I still had this virus but I learned to accept the terms of it. I took a tennis lesson every morning, then I read or rested quietly by the pool. By lunchtime I would feel a little dizzy and by the afternoon I would have to take a nap—maybe an hour or an hour and a half. Then I would get up, play some more tennis and have dinner. In the evening I would run a low-grade fever. I knew it wouldn't turn into anything, and we never broke any plans or missed anything. I took my vitamins faithfully every day and ate fresh and healthy food. I went on for three weeks this way and I started to be filled with hope. I remember being in the bathtub one evening before dinner and I said to Gene, "I don't ever want to leave here—it's the first time in so many months that I've felt well and happy." Of course, to stay at a hotel and not to have to make the bed or cook or shop for groceries—just to relax—certainly helps any illness. It was a glorious vacation.

We spent one evening in Paris before flying back to America. I remember it was very hot, record temperatures for that time of year. The city felt close and steamy and even Sparkle couldn't stop panting in the heat. We ate our dinner at a favorite bistro on the Right Bank near the Louvre. After dinner I got a severe attack of stomach cramps. I'd eaten hardly anything because it was so humid, and there wasn't any air conditioning in the restaurant. My stomach felt bloated and hard. When Gene and I left the bistro, I could barely walk in the streets. There we were in beautiful Paris, with its glorious architecture and romantic avenues, and I was doubled over on the curb waiting for Gene to get a cab. I thought it was nerves because I would soon be flying home, returning home to responsibility. In a few months, *Haunted Honeymoon* was to open and preview screenings hadn't produced much response. There was a screening in Los Angeles, after which nobody called us. With movies you always heard the good news right away. The bad news drifts in slowly. No doubt that was creating a certain amount of stress in me, wondering what had happened at this screening. I'm sure I was thinking that the honeymoon was over and reality was waiting back at home.

When we arrived back in Connecticut, the fog rolled in, this time like a sleeping sickness. I had to spend three days in bed. The stomach cramps continued. There was beginning to be too much wrong with me. On June 28, two weeks after we had come home from France, I turned forty. It's a turning point in anyone's life, but I felt perhaps my life was just beginning. I opened my eyes wide in the bathroom mirror. Without my contacts I have to stand with my nose pressed against the mirror to see. I checked my skin for wrinkles and thought the years didn't look too bad on me. For the first time in months I felt good—actually I felt great, and that alone filled me with hope . . . for the future, for my career, for having a family. *After all,* I thought to myself, *my mother didn't have me until she was forty-one. I'm just a late bloomer.* I thought I had to learn to manage stress better, and to be less neurotic, but everything was possible. I still could have it all.

The phone rang. It was Graciela Daniele, the choreographer who had worked with Dom DeLuise and me on the "Ballin' the Jack" dance number in *Haunted Honeymoon.* She wished me a happy birthday, but said the real reason she had called was that she was thinking about me a lot. She said, "Gilda, you should be dancing. You should be working on things for the stage, the theater. It's what the stage needs right now, a woman like you."

My ears were burning with her confidence in me.

"You're forty years old, and if you don't start doing things now there may not be time. If you want I'll come to you, or you come to New York. You can pick the music of your choice, and we can work on a dance together."

I thought it was wonderful that Graciela was calling me right at that moment. I had wanted to take baby steps toward getting my solo career going again. She thrilled me with the prospect of dancing. I decided right then and there I would make the commitment to go to New York once a week every week and work with her in a studio. I said I already knew the song I wanted to dance to—a song Gene and I loved called "Oh, Babe, What Would You Say?" It was from the early seventies. I used to listen to it on the radio in the first car I ever drove. Hurricane Smith was the artist, and he sang it with such a happy confidence. I wanted to feel that way. Graciela and I made a definite date to meet in New York the following week.

For the rest of my birthday I insisted on playing miniature golf—something I hadn't done since my years of growing up in Detroit. Going on dates and playing miniature golf was very popular in the sixties. I never went on that many dates so I figured on my fortieth birthday I was out with the handsomest guy in the world and that was where I wanted to go—miniature golfing. We went with our neighbors—two couples who live a block away. The course didn't exactly have the windmills and the painted houses and the triple-banked turns I remembered but there was a miniature waterfall, and the girls appropriately lost. Gene gave me a birthday gift. It was a beautiful antique watch fob that had been made into a necklace. The chain was platinum, with little Oriental pearls. It was so beautiful. The card he wrote said, "This is not as loud as your mouth but it's as delicate as your soul, love, your husband."

We spent the next month in Connecticut and New York doing publicity for *Haunted Honeymoon*. Gene did "Good Morning America." I did "Late Night with David Letterman." There were newspaper interviews and press conferences and videotaped talk shows for network affiliates all over the United States. It was exhausting work—anwering the same questions over and over again and trying to make the same answers sound new.

"What's it like working with your husband as your director?"

"Do you miss doing 'Saturday Night Live'?"

"What's next for you?"

At the end of a day, Gene and I were too tired to even talk. As Lorne Michaels, my "Saturday Night Live" producer, used to say, it's part of why they call it "show business"—not "show fun" or "show art."

On July 26, *Haunted Honeymoon* opened nationwide. It was a bomb. One month of publicity and the movie was only in the theaters for a week—a box-office disaster.

4.

The Journey

Show business is like riding a bicycle—when you fall off, the best thing to do is get up, brush yourself off and get back on again. Gene and I mourned *Haunted Honeymoon* together and apart. He went off to London for a week to see plays and fill his head with new ideas. I kept my New York dance schedule, getting my body into shape for the next show ... whatever it would be. The rehearsal studio had a hundred mirrors and I could see myself everywhere in the room. I wore a leotard and a black skirt that swirled when I moved and dancing shoes I hadn't worn since *Gilda Radner Live from New York* was on Broadway, seven years before. You could hear music everywhere in the building. I love the feeling in a rehearsal studio—the creation and anticipation of an opening night.

Somehow my drive, my energy, my adrenaline could rise above what was bothering me physically and mentally. I kept saying to myself, "Take your time, this will go away, you can handle these things." I was free to dance and express myself in any way I wanted, and Graciela began to build a number with me. My music filled the room and we pretended we had sets and a chorus and an audience. I was a star again, reflected everywhere, and my spirit filled the room.

But throughout the summer the pains in my stomach and bowels continued. I went to see my New York gynecologist. She did an exam and said that it was definitely a stomach problem. She suggested that I see a gastroenterologist. I did, and he agreed that I had a stomach problem. I told him about the vitamins I was taking and he felt the high dosages of vitamin C could be causing the gas. He had me go off all the vitamins that I was taking. He was skeptical of the Epstein-Barr virus diagnosis. He thought that my problems were emotional. He had heard that my recent movie hadn't done well. It was the return of the Queen of Neurosis. He felt that most stomach problems were the result of stress and anxiety and could be controlled by getting the stress out of your life. In the past my stomach always had been a stress barometer, so I accepted his diagnosis. He wanted to see me in a couple of weeks after I had discontinued the vitamins and kept a chart of all the foods I was eating so he could find out whether I had some food allergies.

But even while I was having all these health problems, I continued to make progress on my own career. I had always dreamed of being a writer. Since I was a little girl, I had written poetry and short stories—my impressions of the world. I kept journals and revered Emily Dickinson in high school. In college, I found my mouth was mightier than my pen and I chose improvisational comedy and writing on my feet out loud in front of an audience. It trained me later for Second City and "Saturday Night Live," but always inside me was an introspective poet who never was patient enough to write and wait for a response. But I romanticized that writing would be something I could do professionally and still travel anywhere in the world with Gene. I had sent some of my household vignettes to a literary agent. After many rejections from magazines, that same July that *Haunted Honeymoon* bombed, *New Woman* magazine bought some pieces. At the same time *Ms.* magazine was interested in my doing an article. I felt happy, excited that a new career was opening up for me. Now I was going to New York to take my dance classes *and* to see my editors.

Then a new symptom appeared—an aching, gnawing pain in my upper thighs and in my legs. It started slowly, then increased and would not go away. The gynecologist and the gastroenterologist could find no reason for it. My blood work showed nothing wrong. I continued to keep a chart of everything I was eating, and I started to take Tylenol to ease the intense leg pains.

The gastroenterologist decided that I should have a pelvic sonogram to rule out the possibility that any tumor or growth was pressing on a nerve and making my legs ache or causing the bowel disturbance and the gas. The sonogram showed there was some congestion. My ovaries weren't exactly in the place where they were supposed to be, but that wasn't serious. There was no sign of tumor, no sign of an obstruction or a mass, and they sent me home, saying, "Everything is fine—there is nothing to worry about."

I was relieved. I decided I would exercise even more. I walked, I swam, I played tennis and I took lots of Tylenol. I began to notice I was having fewer symptoms of the Epstein-Barr virus—less fatigue. I could go a day without napping. I could exercise without falling apart. The fog didn't seem to come over me as often. Maybe the illness *was* all in my mind. But the dull ache in my legs continued all day and all night.

In the middle of August the gastroenterologist thought my bowel should be checked with a barium enema. A barium enema is one of the true joyous adventures in life. The patient (me) is only allowed to consume liquids for the preceding twenty-four hours. I was given instructions and packets of pills and liquids to take before going to bed the night before. They made me shit my guts out all night long—I don't know how else to say it. I was back and forth to the bathroom until I thought I'd turned my insides out. I felt like a pipe after a Drano treatment.

The next morning I was in a radiology office in New York. The technicians strapped me to a table and then put a tube in my rear end. As they poured a chalky liquid inside me and pumped gas into me so that my bowel would show up in a photograph, they were also turning me slowly around and around on the table so that the barium liquid would go all the way through my bowels, making it possible to get pictures at a lot of different angles.

During my days of "Saturday Night Live," I had been photographed by Scavullo for the cover of *Rolling Stone* and by Richard Avedon for the *Gilda Live* billboard at the

Winter Garden Theatre, but I had never had a photo session quite like this. When I was little I would never go on those rides at amusement parks where you were turned upside down, or the one called "the Rotor" where you stand in a cylinder and the cylinder spins and they take the floor out and you are pressed against the wall. I felt like I was trapped on an endless Ferris wheel with someone's fist up my butt. You can imagine how much I enjoyed the barium enema. I think the word that best captures the whole event is *humiliating*—being photographed spinning with a tube up your ass. All my pictures came out perfect. I had the type of bowel that dipped and turned and had lots of kinks and spinarounds in it, but there were no obstructions, no masses, nothing wrong. Gene and I celebrated with soup and tuna-fish sandwiches on Madison Avenue. At last I had some peace of mind and I could come home happy that I passed that test.

But my leg pains became more intense. Tylenol didn't help. I couldn't sleep at night. I couldn't hold my legs still. I thought I was going crazy. What was wrong with me? The gastroenterologist said he could give me a CAT scan, but he felt it was unnecessary. He suggested I take large doses of anti-inflammatory medication, two pills three or four times a day. It worked, but it caused me to have severe stomach upset—nausea and vomiting. So he prescribed an ulcer medication that stopped the stomach from producing acid. Suddenly I was on two medications just to stop this pain, but all my tests were "normal." I felt like I was going from being Miss Pristine, who wanted to have a baby and was carefully avoiding drugs and chemicals, to becoming a medicine junkie. I had to face the fact that I wasn't well enough to try to have a baby. I would have to wait until I got better to try again. I didn't want to be taking all this medication during pregnancy. Not to mention the fact that chronic pain doesn't make you feel like having sex. In fact, it became the last thing on my mind.

Still, I continued to travel to New York to dance every week and I noticed as I looked at myself in the mirrors that I was getting thinner. I seemed to be getting thinner than I ought to have been. I wasn't on a diet. I didn't feel I was eating less, but my arms were getting very skinny and my face looked drawn and tired. I thought it was probably because I was carrying around pain like a heavy set of luggage. I figured that pain could make you lose weight—trying to keep on going with nagging pain.

Gene spent a lot of time phoning the internist in California, the New York gastroenterologist and the New York gynecologist, and getting prescriptions filled at the pharmacy, hoping the next plan would work and I'd feel well again. He had been offered a movie in Paris. It was a wonderful part for him—shooting was to begin that November. I told him I didn't feel I could go with him. I wanted to stay in the United States and work on my career. Besides, I felt tied to doctors and was frightened of going to Europe and not being in good health. Again, the stress factors were splitting me different ways—the marriage, the baby, the career—but I didn't feel well enough to command the situation. The best Gene and I could do was arrange a schedule so we'd be apart as little as possible.

Being a celebrity can do strange things to the medical attention you get. In some ways it can be very helpful.

Sometimes you can get an appointment faster than some-one else or get a hospital room or maybe a private nurse. Certainly if you have money, you can afford to get more medical attention or a more acclaimed doctor. But the downside of celebrity is that oftentimes you *don't* get the kind of attention that someone who is not a celebrity would get. On one of my doctor visits I took Gene with me, and I saw the doctor get terribly nervous when Gene talked to him. I'm sure he was thinking, *There's the guy from* Young Frankenstein! *There's the guy from* Stir Crazy! He was unable to listen to my symptoms or to really hear what was going on. I have gone to doctors by myself and seen that they are looking at Roseanne Roseannadanna or Emily Litella, and not seeing the person who is sick, who has complaints. They wait, expecting me to be funny. As my symptoms increased, I became less and less funny, more serious, more determined to discover what was wrong with me. I couldn't quit—I knew there was something wrong, and I wasn't going to stop looking for what it was. I knew I may have been neurotic, but I also knew that what was happening to me was real.

On September 15, I took a train by myself from Con-necticut to Boston to see a doctor who had treated over three hundred Epstein-Barr virus patients. When I had spoken to him on the phone to arrange the appointment, he had encouraged me, saying every symptom, even the leg pains I mentioned, he had heard from other Epstein-Barr virus patients. He wanted me to come and see him for an examination. I spent the night in Boston and went to the appointment early in the morning.

He was a lovely man—truly kind, and the first of all the doctors I had seen who really looked into my eyes, who listened to all my complaints. He said he understood; he had heard them before. He was sure this was Epstein-Barr virus. He told me that there was no cure, but that everything I was complaining of was quite normal and I really wasn't in as bad a state as many patients he was seeing. That was encouraging. He wanted me to give a blood sample that they could keep there for experimental research projects. He thought if the medications I was on helped the symptoms, then that was good. He also recommended that I take low dosages of an antidepressant called Elavil. That would help with any sleeping disorder, and a proper night's sleep would help my symptoms, but I would see no effect from the Elavil until I had taken it for two weeks. At this point, I was willing to try anything.

I kept looking searchingly in his eyes for some answer to this, some cure, *something*. I told him I was afraid.

"What is it specifically that you are afraid of?" he asked.

"I am afraid that it is cancer." I had read articles that linked Epstein-Barr virus to blood and lymphatic cancers.

He said, "The best thing you can do is to continue to have your blood work done and continue to stay in contact with a physican so that you set your mind at ease."

When I left his office, I stopped in the lab to give my blood. The technician came out, wrapped the rubber strap around my arm, took my blood, hurriedly took the card that I had filled out and went back to her seat in the laboratory. She had never even looked at me. On my way out, I stopped just around the corner to go to the bathroom. Sitting on the toilet, I realized that I was in the bathroom where you give urine samples, and there was a little box on a door that went directly into the lab.

Through that little door, I could hear the technician yelling at the top of her lungs in the lab, "Oh my God, that was Gilda Radner. I can't believe that she came in here. I didn't say hello. I didn't even look at her. God, this is her blood! I can't believe it."

I just sat there with a smile on my face, thinking, "I hope she doesn't drop it on the floor."

On September 22, I saw my internist in California. My blood work was normal. He suggested I see a new gynecologist, so a week later I saw a California gynecologist. He did a pelvic exam. He felt some scar tissue but everything else appeared normal. He said I could continue trying to have a baby. But I was tired, in pain and running low-grade fevers. I was on too much medication. I decided to see an acupuncturist because friends had begun to suggest alternatives to my medical care. I had never had acupuncture—but I didn't care at this point what I tried. The acupuncturist was a woman. She listened to my medical history and my symptoms patiently. Then she took me into a quiet room and had me lie down on a table. She proceeded to put needles in different places, behind my ears, in my feet and ankes. She was so soothing and healing and patient with me that I loved being there. For a few minutes, lying on that table, I could actually transcend my pain and discomfort because I felt someone cared and I was getting some attention. I became hopeful that this might work. At the same time, when she would leave me alone in the room with all the needles in me, I would think, *What is a Jew doing lying on a table like a chicken about to be basted and put in the oven?*

The pain in my legs was still keeping me from sleeping

at night. Then something went wrong in my bowels and I couldn't go to the bathroom. My stomach started to blow up like a balloon. I looked like a malnourished African baby—skinny arms and legs with a protruding belly. Someone gave me the name of a doctor of holistic medicine so I started to go to a center of holistic medicine where the doctor used a technique developed in Germany. He placed some metal device on pulse points in my body, and it was hooked to something else that showed what I might be allergic to or which vitamins or minerals were missing in my body. He prescribed all this stuff to help me sleep and to help my bowels to move—herbs and roots and things. The German pulse-point system showed some dysfunction in my liver, and he felt I should have more protein in my diet, so he wanted me to take protein supplements. I would painfully drag myself from this holistic medicine center to the health food store across the street to get protein concoctions. Then he wanted me to give myself coffee enemas. I went from drugstore to drugstore trying to find the right kind of enema bag for coffee enemas. I had what seemed like hundreds of little pills and bottles, holistic drops and bags of seeds and leaves and cans of food supplements, all accompanied by rigorous schedules of when to take and do what. But this holistic doctor was paying attention to me. He called me every day and asked how I felt, and what's going on, and is this working, and let's change this. At least he and the acupuncturist were taking me seriously.

Gene felt helpless. We didn't go out. He did all the grocery shopping and the cooking. I vaguely remember watching the World Series on TV that October, doubled up in pain on the couch.

On October 13 the acupuncturist stuck needles in my swollen stomach and gave me a special abdominal massage. Two days later, the holistic doctor suggested I have a colonic to clean out the bowel. I insisted that would be too weird for me. The next day, I saw my internist. He did blood work again—I was running a low-grade fever. He gave me a gamma globulin shot, which was working on some patients with this Epstein-Barr virus. He felt my stomach and told me I was literally "full of shit," and gave me a prescription for laxatives. He said to come back in a week.

Suddenly I began to wonder how to please so many people. Do I take the magnesium citrate? What about the coffee enema? Do I do both? Do I do the abdominal massage or the colonic? Do I tell the doctors about each other? East meets West in Gilda's body: Western medicine down my throat, Eastern medicine up my butt.

The holistic doctor was paying the most attention to me, so on October 17 I went to get a professional colonic. I had reached a point where the pain and the discomfort, including not being able to get my pants done up, had gone too far. I went to someone in Beverly Hills who gives colonics. I was so ill at this point that the holistic doctor's assistant drove me there. I remember this like a foggy dream. She took me to the office and waited like mother in the waiting room. It's a weird procedure, like a big enema—water pours into you while your stomach is massaged. You lie on a table with a clear tube alongside you. You can see water flowing in and out, so any material that is removed from the bowel passes by. I will never forget looking past my swollen stomach at the tube, and the only thing that floated by was a bean sprout. Just a single bean sprout went by. I guess they're difficult to digest.

5.

The Hospital

My health continued to deteriorate. I managed to go to the post office and wait in line with my bloated belly and skinny arms to buy a hundred aerograms so I could write to Gene every day in France. He was scheduled to leave to make his movie on October 30. His clothes had been shipped ahead. A friend was coming to live in our guest cottage so I wouldn't be alone. On Monday, October 20, 1986, in the late afternoon, I had just come home from my psychiatrist's appointment. I was in a lot of pain, but I was still driving and trying to keep up with life. The phone rang; it was the internist. He said my blood work from the previous week showed an irregularity in my liver function tests.

"What does that mean?" I screeched into the phone.

"It can mean something—or nothing. It's only slight and we'll recheck you Thursday when you come in."

"But what does it mean?" I persisted.

"Relax, Gilda. We'll recheck it. It's probably nothing."

"If it's nothing, why did you call?"

"Well, we have to recheck it."

I was petrified that night. Gene held me, talked to me and finally got me to take something to sleep.

On Tuesday, October 21, I drove to see the holistic doctor. He put me on a special powdered protein diet. I canceled my acupuncture appointment. The next day, I canceled my appointment for another colonic. I was in too much pain even to leave the house. On Thursday, October 23, Gene's secretary drove me to see the internist. My stomach was inflated like a balloon and I was too weak to drive myself. The internist did a pelvic exam. He checked me into the hospital immediately for tests.

There is a VIP wing at the hospital, six rooms that are luxuriously appointed. My room was carpeted and had upholstered furniture. It was decorated in what I think of as a Jewish-Chinese motif—burgundy and pink sofas and chairs and oriental tchotchkes on the coffee table. It was equipped with a television, a VCR, a radio and a tape player. It could have been a hotel suite if it weren't for the hospital bed and examining lights occupying one corner. A nurse came in and took my blood pressure and temperature and gave me a hospital gown. I had a slight smile because I thought, *At last, somebody believes me.* I was done with the day-to-day world. I could no longer manage even simple tasks. I had to be taken care of, but I felt, *At last, somebody believes me. Someone will find out what's wrong.* I put on the little blue print gown. I wanted to get into bed, but they wanted to start their diagnostic procedures right away.

They took me downstairs to the radiation department and began running numerous tests on me. Blood was drawn. I had an ultrasound—to make sure I wasn't pregnant. I wasn't. Then came the CAT scan. The internist was there overseeing everything. I had never had a CAT scan or anything like it in my life. The closest I ever came was when I saw the Woody Allen movie *Hannah and Her Sisters*. That movie did so much for me because I saw it right in the middle of all my weird illness and it confirmed the results of neurosis for me. I thought about how Woody created his brain tumor. Good old Woody, he hit right on what's happening in my life, too, that this whole thing could be me just being neurotic. Except this wasn't a movie. It was really happening. It was my body going through the round eye of the CAT-scan machine. I became like a child. I put myself in other people's hands.

Gene was in my room when I got back. He was calm and reassuring. "Now we'll get to the bottom of this," he said. At this point we were both exhausted from trying to figure out why I felt so ill. Our daily life had become painful. We needed help.

The first night I had a private nurse named Bonnie. She was single and my age exactly. She kept track of my vital signs and gave me enemas every half hour. I was hooked up to an intravenous line for feeding—nothing by mouth. After Gene had gone home, Bonnie and I put on the television and there was a rerun of "Saturday Night Live." Bonnie had never seen me on television before. She told me she preferred the night shift in the hospital, working a twelve-hour shift from 7:00 P.M. to

7:00 A.M. When she wasn't working, she liked dancing at clubs. She loved movies and music, but television wasn't very important to her. She had only a small black-and-white set at home. Now, there she was—giving enemas to this person who was on color television at the same time. We laughed about it. Bonnie gave me a sleeping medication. I didn't even ask what it was. I felt strangely content—I was being taken care of.

Friday morning, fluid was extracted from my swollen belly. I was taken downstairs again for more tests—chest X-rays and a mammogram. Gene was in the room again when I got back. My psychiatrist paid a visit. We all thought this was probably some kind of infection. I remember feeling calm, which isn't like me, so I must've been sedated.

In the late afternoon or early evening on Friday, the internist came into the room. I was lying in the bed and Gene was sitting on the left side of my bed. We had been talking, absently watching television, waiting for the reports to come in. We both looked up into this doctor's eyes as he said, very calmly, "We've discovered there is a malignancy." A flush went through my body, and out of my mouth came a sound like a guttural animal cry. Gene said he did the same thing, but silently. He still remembers the sound I made because it was so primitive, so emotional, like somebody stabbing a knife into me. What about Epstein-Barr virus and neurosis and Woody Allen and my imagination? I think the internist went on to say that the malignancy was confirmed by the CAT scan and the analysis of the fluid from my belly. Surgery would have to be done as soon as possible. When he left the room, I grabbed Gene's face in my hands and sobbed.

"No more bad news, no more bad news, please! I just don't want any more bad news."

I can't remember much after that. I don't remember being horrified or dwelling on it—whether it was because they were medicating me at that point, I don't know. Everything happened quickly from that Friday night until they operated on me Sunday morning. Saturday I was prepped for surgery and Gene says I met the anesthesiologist and the gynecologist who was to perform the operation. I don't remember anything. I was probably filled with medication that dripped through my intravenous line. I do remember that nobody said the word *cancer*.

After the surgery I woke up, I was in the intensive care unit and Gene was right there. My eyes opened and his face was right there. He said, "They got it all. They got everything they could see. They got you clean."

"Oh, my husband—my dear, sweet husband," I said.

We held onto each other.

But I developed a fever that night as high as 104 degrees. I also developed pneumonia. I was kept in the intensive care unit for five days. I have only a vague memory of those days, in and out of sleep with nurses' arms and faces around me in what I refer to as "the bin," a grown-up crib for the very ill. The fever finally went down. Unknown to me, Gene was facing another battle at the same time, one that illustrates the darker side of being a celebrity.

From the minute I checked into the hospital certain segments of the press were trying to find out what was going on. Journalists were calling and asking what room Gilda Radner was in. Gene had to change my name on all the medical records. I became Lily Herman. I had always wanted to name our first girl Lily, and my father's name was Herman. The *Enquirer* found out my new name and published it, so calls started to come in for Lily Herman. The *Enquirer* had chosen me for their cover story: GILDA RADNER IN LIFE-DEATH STRUGGLE. In their story, I was dying and Gene was supposed to do a movie in France, and the question was, would he go or would he stay? They found an old photo of me looking frightened from a "Saturday Night Live" sketch and blew that up to make the point. What they did probably sold newspapers, but it had a devastating effect on my family and my friends. It forced Gene to compose a press release to respond. He said that I had been diagnosed with ovarian cancer, had had surgery and my prognosis was good.

The *Enquirer* doesn't like good news, so the Gilda story stopped running. A hospital coordinator changed our names to Lorna and Stanley Blake. Every morning the man who took my blood greeted me with "Good morning, Lorna."

My surgery involved a total hysterectomy. I would never have a baby. Everything had happened so fast. I hadn't even realized before the operation that it would probably involve the removal of my reproductive organs. When they told me afterward, I understood the issue was to save my life. There was nothing to say. No more biological time clock to worry about. The important thing was that I was alive.

Immediately after the surgery an oncologist told us I would have to have nine courses of chemotherapy, one every three weeks, and he would give me the first treatment before I left the hospital once I was strong enough.

I decided to call him "the Alchemist" because he decided which chemicals or drugs to administer, and in what doses, to treat the cancer. He also insisted that I have some kind of relaxation therapy. He knew that an important part of cancer treatment was the mental attitude of the patient and the patient's ability to accept the treatment and to relax during it. I already had a psychiatrist, but he suggested I meet with a woman named Joanna Bull, a psychotherapist who worked primarily with cancer patients and was skilled in relaxation therapies. Within the first ten days of my recuperation I had an appointment to see her. She would come to the hospital to meet me. The Alchemist understood that he was treating the mind as well as the body.

I had private nurses around the clock in twelve-hour shifts. Not only did I need them medically, but I needed the protection within the hospital—like a guard. That made it easier on Gene and everybody else, knowing that somebody was there with me. And there were other doctors who entered the case. One was a doctor who decided what went into the feeding bag that dripped into my veins. I would wake up in the morning and he would be the first one I would see, standing there fixing my feed bag, deciding what balance of nutrients I needed.

The doctors decided that the veins in my arms were not easily accessible, which wouldn't be good for my chemotherapy. They would have to put the chemicals in my veins, but it would be difficult to keep finding a vein to put an IV in. Fortunately there is an amazing new invention called a Port-A-Cath. It's like a small plastic bottle with a long wire neck that runs into a vein. It is put under your skin surgically like a pacemaker, usually in the chest area. Once it is in place, to give you an IV they just stick the needle into the Port-A-Cath, which hurts much less than sticking the vein. You can do anything with it, even go swimming with it. At first, Port-A-Caths were open and you would have to clean them all the time, but now they are covered over with skin and very safe and less likely to get infected. I have mine to this day, above my right breast. So eleven days after my initial operation, I had to go back down to surgery to have the Port-A-Cath inserted.

I spent three weeks in the hospital. Though I'd had major surgery for removal of a grapefruit-sized tumor, a complete hysterectomy and a scraping of many of my internal organs, I spent the first week out of intensive care in a dreamy state of happiness. I was on a very potent painkiller called Dilaudid which kept me stoned out and calm. I remember I spent one whole day watching a lamp. I thought it was the television set. I could hear the television set in the background, but I watched the lamp and I was quite content. It never entered my mind that there was no picture and it wasn't worth moving where my head was, so I just stared at the lamp all day. I would make phone calls to people I knew—to my childhood friend Judy, to my other good friends and to my mother and brother. I was happy and I was very eager to tell everyone I was all right. So I talked to the people closest to me during that time, and made jokes and laughed.

They weaned me off the Dilaudid, but I had an awful withdrawal. I spent two nights with sweats and chills. I became anxious, paranoid, on edge. I hated everybody. I didn't want to make any phone calls. When the Alchemist phoned to see how I was doing, I told him I hated him and never wanted to see him again. I told my night nurse that I was mean and she should just do her job and not talk to me. I phoned Gene and told him not to come and visit me. Fortunately everyone realized that the medication was influencing my behavior. But coming off the pain medication was one of the hardest parts of the whole recuperation.

Gradually my spirit revived. I knew I had to take one step at a time to get well. I am good with strangers so when a new nurse came in, I would make her laugh and want her to like me. It was psychologically good for me to have round-the-clock nurses. I remember them, and owe a great deal to them. I don't think they get enough credit for what they do in terms of passing spirit along. They were all concerned with me being relaxed, and all of them, of course, knew more about me than I did, from reading my charts.

One nurse would bring me relaxation tapes or the soundtrack from *Out of Africa* to listen to because I wasn't sleeping well at night. I would be listening to the *Out of Africa* tape and pretending I was just falling asleep when suddenly I'd say, "Is this the part where Robert Redford crashes the airplane?" and she'd jump up and say, "Why aren't you asleep?"

Another nurse had this incredible punk, spiked haircut. When you touched it you could cut yourself on the points. I decided I wanted my hair cut that way. One of my day nurses drew a picture of how it could look and the next day I got a hairdresser friend to come and cut my hair. I also asked to have a manicure and a pedicure and someone came and gave me those. Sometimes that would be the only event of the day, or a sponge bath, or getting my legs shaved, but I always had some life force, some activity, going on.

I was always hungry for news from my nurses—tell me about your life; are you dating anybody? One nurse was single and would tell me all these incredible stories of her going after guys in rock bands and having affairs in the backs of cars and good, dirty stuff like that. Another had a boyfriend who was trying to be a stand-up comic so she would tell me about her adventures going to nightclubs, trying to help him in his career. Of course, I had lots of advice in that department.

I took it all in. I wanted to know everything. Usually I would be seeing them again so I wanted to know the next installment. I was even a little happy, despite the cancer and all. I don't know why I was happy except that I found out I have a very strong spirit, a powerful will to live. In the hospital, it never entered my mind that I wouldn't live. I just had to take one step at a time.

Every day I would walk around my floor and put chalk marks on a blackboard at one end of the hall to note how many times I had walked around. There was an older man with stomach problems who was there the whole time I was there. He was always watching sports in his room, and I would go in and make bets on the games with him. He'd make bets on how many times I could walk around the floor. I saw that I could make the best out of the situation at hand—that I was someone who said, "This is what I have, this is my world now, so make the best out of that world." I watched myself on "Saturday Night Live" reruns, young and alive. I looked healthy and

I wanted to be that way again. I became my own audience.

Gene came every day and sneaked Sparkle in with him. He said that if anybody was going to stop him, he would say he bought her at the gift shop and she ran on batteries. So I got to see my Sparkle.

Gene would go shopping in Beverly Hills and bring me beautiful things in boxes like you would see in the old movies, with big bows on them that you could take off with one pull—like Tiffany's. I'd just pull the string and the bow would come open and in the box would be a new nightgown or a new robe. It was joyful every time he appeared in the doorway bringing gifts and messages from the outside world. Gene became funnier than I have ever seen him. He is very funny in the movies but he's not that funny in real life. He's shy. He's a comic actor as opposed to a comedian. I think I am a comedienne—a performer, an entertainer, where he is an actor. But he became very funny, telling stories around my bed, assisting the nurses like Dr. Frankenstein, holding a flashlight for intricate procedures and shaking it on purpose like he was nervous.

I became mischievous myself. I liked walking as fast as I could while Gene was pushing my IV stand, so he couldn't keep up with me. That would make me laugh so hard. It was dumb stuff, but it would make me laugh that I could walk faster than he could push my IV bottle. The nurse couldn't keep up with me either. The truth was, they were putting me on. Anyone could have gone faster than me. But I was just like a child. I felt like Eloise, the fictional little girl who lived at the Plaza Hotel in New

York. Gene would have his dinner in the hospital with me every night. I didn't eat for a month, but after he ate he'd lie in bed with me and we'd talk or watch TV. I would cry as easily as I'd laugh.

Sometimes I would even lie in my bed and think up things to make people laugh on purpose. Like, I'd wait till the nurse left the room—maybe she had just gone into the hall to get a coffee or get her lunch—and then I'd buzz for her and say into the intercom, "Nurse," in the most pathetic way possible. "Nurrrsseee." I always got them laughing that way. It was some strange form of "The Judy Miller Show"—the hyperkinetic child's fantasy I did on "Saturday Night Live." In this protected environment, I was still the clown, still wanting to be liked . . . to be loved . . . to be funny . . . to perform.

Late one afternoon, not quite two weeks after my surgery, I had my first appointment with Joanna Bull. Joanna was in her late forties. Her face was round and open and her blond hair was cut in a Buster Brown style. It was as though an angel had walked into my hospital room, an angel filled with life. I never saw anybody like her; I never saw anybody with so much spirit. She flew into the room, plopped herself *fearlessly* at the foot of my bed and put her arms on my legs so there was a physical contact between us. She talked to me about cancer. She was a psychotherapist who worked at a place called The Wellness Community, where she was assistant director. She counseled cancer patients all the time, and she was just sparkly. I remember her sparkling eyes. We talked about cancer, specifically about my feelings about it. I told her that I thought this ordeal was a school I was going through, that I was meant to teach and help others.

She said that now it was more important to see this as an "exquisite" time to take care of myself and heal my own body. We talked about the upcoming chemotherapy. She knew I was seeing a psychiatrist at the time and she said she was assigned not to deal with my psychological problems but to help me learn to relax and to handle having cancer.

I protested that I had *had* cancer. But Joanna confronted me with the fact that you never know. She herself has a form of leukemia. She has no symptoms and it may stay in remission all of her life, or it may show up at any moment. She lives with cancer all the time. That made me trust her. I had a lot of months of treatment ahead of me. The important thing was that I learn to make that treatment work for me in the best way physically and in the best way psychologically, and to use techniques of visualization and relaxation to imagine I was helping the chemicals fight the cancer cells. She put me through a relaxation exercise so I could learn to kind of transcend my body and the feelings in it to a mental state of well-being. Then she had me do visualization throughout my body, concentrating on health and getting well. It was hard to do at first, but she came back three times a week in the hospital, then she came to my house after I was home.

Joanna would speak in a slow, even, delicious voice. I would lie there in bed and she would talk me through a series of motions. telling me to tense my body in all different areas so that I could get a sense of the difference between being tense and being relaxed. "Tighten up your toes and curl them up as hard as you can, then release them and let them go." Then she woul through my whole body one part at a time until my entire body was relaxed. She would lead my conscious mind through other exercises—relaxation and healing, putting light in certain areas, healing light; seeing the word *relax*, seeing it far away and closer. These were drills for my conscious mind to help my body to relax. I was going down a stairway into deeper and deeper relaxation. After doing this four or five times, I began to realize this was meditation. I also found that even though I fought it, I would go into this relaxation feeling that Joanna was talking about. The sound of her voice was very soothing, and during our sessions, even if only for twenty-five minutes or half an hour, instead of being in the hospital room with tubes and doctors and stress and blood tests and X-rays, I would feel as though I had been somewhere, on a trip out of the world.

The most important thing Joanna ever said to me was, "You can't do anything wrong when you are doing this technique. There is no wrong." Like for a second I'd start to think about something else, or a thought would shoot into my mind like, *Is the dog getting her bath today?*— that was okay. It didn't mean I had ruined it—it didn't mean it wasn't working. If I wanted to stop in the middle and say, "Look, I feel too edgy—this isn't working right at this minute"—that was okay. Joanna said, "There is no wrong; you find what works for you." When she gave relaxation no rules, she made it possible for me to keep trying. "If you lose track and go off into thinking about something else, bring yourself back. That is part of the exercise. Bring yourself back to relaxation." This was the most freeing thing to me, that there was no right or wrong.

Because my life was always stressful, a lot of people had told me that I should meditate. I thought meditation was some weird Indian yogi thing, and the only yogi I ever knew was somebody who could put a rope through his nose and make it come out his bum. I thought that was interesting but not something I wanted to do. I had heard about mantras and all that, but all I could think of was I would have to take my contact lenses out to do that because I can't keep my eyes closed that long with them in; they start to hurt. It's hard enough to put them in in the morning without taking them out for forty-five minutes and then putting them back in. So, instead, I continued with my stressful life.

But Joanna told me right away that, in order to participate in battling cancer and to help the chemotherapy work, it's very important to be relaxed and to have times of relaxation when your mind can let your body go so that it can work on healing itself. She also told me that there are techniques of visualizing the healing, visualizing the chemicals going into your body and working to fight the cancer cells. And if you visualize the cancer cells and see them as evil and visualize them being removed from your body, you are supporting the actual process.

What I didn't know during this time in the hospital was that I didn't have just ovarian cancer. It had spread to my bowel and my liver, but the cells hadn't eaten into those organs. They were just lying on top of those organs, so the doctors had removed all the cancer they could see. The internist told Gene that I had only a twenty-percent chance of survival and that they would not know until I was two months into chemotherapy whether or not I would survive. It depended entirely on whether I responded to this particular chemotherapy. Gene, of course, never told me, but he was carrying that information all the time behind his smiling face. Not surviving never entered my head at all. Even today I feel so awful for Gene that he was carrying that load and he couldn't let on to me.

The Alchemist wanted to begin my chemotherapy as quickly as possible. Ovarian cancer is often extremely fast-growing. It's very insidious. All of a woman's major organs are down there in the same cavity, so even though the primary location of the cancer was the ovary, it was jumping onto the other organs. The surgeons thought they had removed all the cancer cells, but there could be microscopic cancer cells that couldn't be seen with the human eye. That is why they needed to do chemotherapy as soon as possible, before the cells could spread.

On November 11, I lay on my hospital bed like a Muppet and received my first chemotherapy. I tried to do my meditation, to relax as Joanna had taught me, but soon I was heavily medicated into a deep sleep while the drugs were dripped into my IV Port-A-Cath. It seemed like just another of the many procedures that had been done to me. I wasn't sick; I was just asleep. I woke up thirty-six hours later, weird and wired, and went home.

During my entire stay in the hospital I had not once seen my reflection. There was no mirror, except in the bathroom, but it was so much work to get to the bathroom that I didn't bother to stand and look in the mirror. When I went home, I saw myself reflected in my own mirror in my own room. A horror came over me—total horror—because I weighed ninety-five pounds. I had no rear end at all. I couldn't sit in the bathtub. I had to put a towel down because the bones would stick out and hit the bottom. There were huge circles under my eyes and I was as thin as anyone you ever saw in documentary footage of Auschwitz. I looked like I was going to die. It was the first time I was frightened. It was the first time I actually feared what might happen to me—what *was* happening to me. Who was that person in that mirror? Whose image was reflected? This is a nightmare. Why me? This is *cancer!* I am only forty years old, and I could die.

6.
Cancer

My father, Herman, was a tremendously powerful businessman who had an extraordinary personality. When he walked into a room the energy in the room changed. He had a zip in his step and a twinkle in his eye and although he had never set foot on a stage in his life, he had the presence of somebody in show business.

My father had a huge family that he was the star of . . . eleven brothers and sisters. He grew up on New York's Lower East Side and never went past fifth grade in school. He could barely write, but he knew about money and business and property, and he was one of those American success stories that proved you could make it on sheer ingenuity. When he was a teenager in the early 1900s, his family moved from New York to Detroit, Michigan. He hung out in a local pool hall and hustled until he got enough money together with friends to buy the pool hall. By the 1920s he was able to buy a brewery in Windsor, Canada, just across the river from Detroit. It was called the Walkerville Brewery and it made whiskey and beer. This was the era of Prohibition. No one in the family talks about it very much and they won't tell me for sure, but it's obvious to me that you were allowed to make and export beer in Canada during Prohibition. I know my father came out of the 1930s with a lot of money, and there is a story about how some people tried to kidnap him once in a dark alley and he was shot in the leg getting away. Now I don't know if we are talking organized crime or what, but he was a pretty happening guy. In his heyday, Herman Radner had a scrapbook full of newspaper articles about himself. He turned his brewery into a free lunchroom during the Depression and fed thousands of people, and there were stories about that everywhere. However he made his money, he spent the rest of his life giving back. He was very active in Jewish affairs and the Jewish old folks' home in Detroit. I remember my father was listed in a book called *Who's Who in American Jewry,* which called him a Detroit philanthropist. It also mentioned that he had changed the family name to Radner from Ratkowsky.

On November 29, 1937, Herman Radner married a beautiful legal secretary named Henrietta Dworkin. Four years later, Henrietta gave birth to a son, Michael. Five years after that they produced me. I came around late in my father's life. I wasn't born until he was fifty-three.

When I was twelve years old, my father went into the hospital for some routine tests. He had been having terrible headaches for a couple of years. He had his glasses changed a hundred times and tried different medications, but the headaches didn't go away. He was in the hospital only two nights, but as far as I was concerned, I never saw him again. They opened him up, found a malignant brain tumor that was too far gone to remove and closed him up again. Besides having brain surgery, he had a stroke that paralyzed the left side of his body. Two days later I was taken to see my father: the bubbly, slightly overweight, middle-aged man who called me "his heart." What I saw was a severely ill old man. He was sixty-five, but he seemed to have aged twenty years. His head had been shaved and the stroke had weakened and confused him. My family said, "That's your father." "That's your father." I was frozen in fear and confusion. He looked like my father. He spoke to me, and I stood there, and I held his hand beside his bed, but it had happened too suddenly. It was too great and sudden a loss of a person whom I adored, and who adored me. I know about the sudden loss of someone who just drops dead of a heart attack, but there was something even weirder about this. The person disappeared but the shell was still there. The brain surgery and the stroke changed his personality, his attitudes and his moods forever.

The doctors put him on a program of radiation therapy because that is how they were treating brain tumors. It must have been 1958 because I was twelve. I don't believe there was chemotherapy at that time, and even today doctors don't use chemotherapy to treat all brain tumors. He did recover from the surgery to the extent that he relearned to use the left side of his body through exercise and concentration. He was very ill from the radiation, very nauseous and sick all the time, but after recuperating in the hospital for a few months, he did come home. I remember going to visit him in the hospital and everyone pretended he was all right. It was like "The Emperor's New Clothes." Nobody ever said the word *cancer*.

My father owned and operated an apartment hotel in downtown Detroit called the Seville. It was his pride and joy. It had a restaurant and a drugstore and a barbershop. When he got sick, he never went to the hotel anymore and his brothers sold it. It disappeared just like he did.

For two years my father was home. During that time he was very ill. It was not unusual in the middle of the night for me to hear the ambulance coming down our street. I would be in my room and would hear the men coming up the stairs with the stretcher. I'd hear them talk to my father like he was a little boy, "Come on, fella—get on the stretcher—that's a good boy." I'd lie in my bed with feelings of anger and resentment, not understanding what was going on and never really getting a clear explanation from anybody. Even today when there is cancer in the family, everybody lies about what is going on. Children especially don't get clear answers.

After my father came home, it seemed like there was something about me in particular that would upset him. I was so young and I think he knew he wasn't going to be around long. Every time he saw me he would become emotional and well up with tears, I imagine because he had had me so late in life and he knew he wasn't going to see me grow up. I only wondered, *Why is he so weak? Why is he crying all the time?* I was angry instead of compassionate, as an older person probably would have been. I know that I have to forgive myself for being ashamed of him because he looked so old and not wanting my friends to see him. I went to camp the summer after he came home and my mother brought him to visit. All the kids said, "Is that your grandfather?"

I said, "It's my father."

"What's wrong with him?"

"Well, he was very sick—he had an operation."

"Is he going to get better?"

"I don't know."

In his last six months, my father went into a coma. He was in the hospital just barely alive; only his heart was still beating. I didn't want to go visit him, but periodically I would go. It was just his body lying there—attached to machines, his heart beating.

I was back at camp the next summer. It was August. I was sound asleep when someone tapped me. I woke up with the owner of the camp looking at me. It was early in the morning, and he said, "Gilda, your mother called, and your father has taken a turn for the worse. Your mother would like you to come home." I got up out of my bed. All of my camp friends were in their bunks. I got dressed, packed, and they all were sitting up staring at me. I kissed everyone goodbye and then went to the camp kitchen and waited. My counselor went with me so I wouldn't be alone. A small plane flew me back to Detroit where my brother was waiting for me at the airport. I was fourteen, my brother almost nineteen. I knew my father was dead. I knew there could be no turn for the worse. My brother took my hand in the car, which brothers and sisters don't usually do, and we didn't talk very much while he drove.

Our house felt like it had just taken a sigh of relief. There had been illness in it for so long and uncertainty and a sense of death. The house was finally relaxed. The windows were open and there was a breeze coming through. My mother seemed relieved. She had been through a hard time. She had been wonderful through it all because my father took a lot out on her during the illness. He was irrationally angry at her a lot. But she stayed right in there, and when he could go out, she went out, and was proud to have him by her side. There was a funeral and in the Jewish religion you sit *shiva* for a week, which I did. Then I went back to camp because I wanted to. I was young and it was a very difficult time. I never got an appropriate mourning period. I spent years trying to mourn my father's death properly through psycho-analysis and psychotherapy. It was a very hard thing for me to understand. I was only a child.

Twelve years old is the age when sexuality is just coming into your life—puberty and getting your period, and all kinds of things happening to your body that seem out of control. It's such a strange time. To be losing a parent at that age as well can make you feel helpless. My family could have probably used some help in living with the illness. Now, almost thirty years later, my mother, my brother and I are still suffering from that illness, that cancer that killed my father.

As far as I know, no one else in my father's large family died of cancer. His mother, Molly, died of a heart attack before I was born. Her husband, George, my grandfather, died of a heart attack in his late eighties. My mother's father, Alfred, lived long into his nineties and died of old age. But cancer is very much a part of my mother's maternal family.

My mother's mother, Golda, died in her early sixties of stomach cancer while my mother was pregnant with me. I was named after my grandmother whose name began with *G*, but "Gilda" came directly from the movie with Glenn Ford and Rita Hayworth.

Then in 1974, my mother was diagnosed with breast cancer. At the time it seemed that not so many women had breast cancer. But this was pre–Betty Ford, and I now realize that a lot of women had breast cancer but they didn't talk about it. It was devastating to my mother. She had not dated much since my father died, but had just started seeing a man she liked. She was feeling very happy and good about herself, and then she discovered the lump. At that time they did radical mastectomies right away. There was no other choice. I don't believe she had any chemotherapy, but a few years later in a checkup they found that some of that breast cancer had metastasized to her lung. It was operable, and they took out a lot of her lung and put her on a pill form of chemotherapy for a while. Today my mother is eighty-four years old and she has never had any recurrence of cancer. She never had reconstructive breast surgery, but in between the two cancer operations she had a face-lift. I think that may be the reason she is still around, that drive to look good and be well. When Betty Ford came out and spoke publicly about her mastectomy, it definitely helped people like my mother adjust. My mother handled cancer well. She went right on with her life.

Ten years before my mother's bout with breast cancer, I had a suspicious lump removed from my right breast. I was eighteen years old and it was the summer before my freshman year in college. The doctor drew with a pencil on my breast where the lump was. I came home and my mother cried and her two sisters cried, and I didn't know why they were crying. The doctors kept feeling the lump and sending me to other doctors to feel the lump and then decided to do surgery. I checked into a Detroit hospital. When they wheeled me into surgery, my mother was crying, but I wasn't. I guess I didn't really understand what was happening. I thought they were going to go in and take this lump out, that's all. After the surgery, I woke up and there was a big bandage over my right breast. A lady came into my room when I was just waking up and said, "I am so happy for you. I wasn't so lucky—I lost my breast." I thought, *What is she talking about? What's going on here?* I just didn't understand the possible consequences of breast cancer.

The lump turned out to be a benign cyst. It was almost unheard of to have breast cancer at age eighteen. I recuperated very quickly. Later I found out that the particular doctor who had done my surgery lost his license for doing unnecessary surgery on women. Whether I was a victim of that or not, I don't know. I also found out I was very cystic and around my period I would get fibroid breast cysts all the time. That may have been what my lump was. The surgeon made an incision that left an ugly scar. That scar kept the fear of cancer marked on my body and my mind.

A few years after my mother's breast cancer, her sister, Elsie, died of stomach cancer just like their mother,

Golda. Elsie was also in her early sixties and got minimal benefit from the chemotherapy that was then available. She left a son and two daughters. The younger daughter, Lenore, has battled cancer three times since her mother's death, beginning when she was forty years old—in both breasts, and then, ten years later, in her ovaries. She is in her fifties now and has fought like a commando and conquered it all three times. She has been a shining example to me, especially being in my family and probably having the same genes—the ones that make us prone to getting the disesase and the ones that make us prone to getting well again. Lenore told me to hang on to the fact that I would be well again, that my illness was temporary. All through her treatments she had continued her aerobics classes and kept herself beautiful. She encouraged me to keep living a healthy life.

In 1976, after completing my first year on "Saturday Night Live," after we knew the show was a success, I had a routine exam with my gynecologist. He felt a cyst in my ovary and put me in the hospital immediately. I had major surgery again. It all happened so quickly that there wasn't even time to think about cancer. I was fifteen pounds lighter when I began my second season on "Saturday Night Live." The fact that later the cancer I got turned out to be ovarian didn't come as a total surprise to me. I was always cystic there and had had problems with that.

Medical experts—scientists and researchers—claim that even though our genetics can predispose us to cancer, it takes the addition of other variables like environment, including what we eat and drink and breathe, to generate the disease. I had thought that I was neurotically afraid of "the big C." It certainly was always around in my family. Even my astrological sign is Cancer. But I would walk out of my way to avoid passing a sign in a building that had the word *cancer* on it. The word jumped into my face from newspapers and magazines—and kept ringing in my ears after it was said. I may have been genetically predisposed to cancer, but I wonder what the variables were in my life that added to this predisposition. Why me? Since cancer is an illness in which your body is out of control, your natural instinct is to want to control it. It runs through my mind constantly: *Why did I get this?* I go from being realistic to being absurd. I wonder, *What did I do wrong? What did I do in my life that would cause this?*

In my case, I know I used a lot of saccharin and cyclamates in my life. I would put those tablets in my coffee in the morning to make it really sweet. I had some kind of artificial sweetener that I got from Canada when they took it off the market in the U.S. because it was a suspected carcinogen. My father smuggled beer into the United States; I smuggled cyclamates. I used them in cooking and I was drinking Tab besides. I was heavy into saccharin and cyclamates for over twenty years.

I smoked. I started smoking when I was fourteen. I thought it was the coolest thing anyone could possibly do. I remember going on an airplane to New York with my girlfriend Ellen, the summer before high school. We both smoked, and I said to her, "If we're going to smoke, don't let us both smoke at the same time. It'll look more mature if only one person smokes at a time." I'm sure it must have looked disgusting to see two little girls sitting on an airplane smoking cigarettes. My girlfriends tell me when I first smoked, I went cross-eyed when I inhaled because I was trying to see the cigarette and see how good I looked smoking. I loved to smoke. It gave me an identity. It was a way to end a meal, a conversation, an event. It was an exclamation point in my life that I thought could just keep going. (I managed to cut down on my smoking later, but I didn't quit completely until my cancer diagnosis.)

I have always loved red candies. I was like a Red Dye #2 junkie. Red licorice, jelly beans, lollipops—you name it. If there was a choice, I always ate the red candies. I was packing them away all those years. Even when I heard that Red Dye #2 was carcinogenic I still would go for them.

For me, the cancer-causing list continues. I have always been a compulsive consumer. I chewed a tremendous amount of gum—sugarless bubble gum by the case. I consumed boxes of chocolate-covered peanuts—not the small bags, but the boxes. I ate an apple a day—even the ones that were thick-skinned with shiny wax. I have eaten tuna for lunch almost every day of my life since I could chew. Could it have been the tuna?

I have lived in New York and I have even lived in Los Angeles, so I have breathed infinite quantities of unhealthy air. I barbecued every Memorial Day weekend in my life, every Fourth of July, every Labor Day and every Sunday in the summer. Gene loves to barbecue too. I have heard you aren't supposed to eat burnt food—anything burnt is carcinogenic—and I love burnt stuff. These are the things that run through my head, from the sensible to the ridiculous. I ate red meat. I used hairspray.

Whatever the American Cancer Society says causes cancer, I have undoubtedly done it. I know the key to a healthy life is moderation, and I have never been moderate. For example, I coped with stress by having every possible eating disorder from the time I was nine years old. I have weighed as much as 160 pounds and as little as 93. When I was a kid, I overate constantly. My weight distressed my mother and she took me to a doctor who put me on Dexedrine diet pills when I was ten years old. They caused me to have tremendous mood swings and I had to discontinue using them. Throughout my teenage years stress caused me to overeat and the fear of being fat put me on tedious and endless diets. I have read every diet book ever written and I know the caloric content of any food by heart. Any emotion could drive me into binge eating that would be followed by days of rigorous dieting.

With fame and the constant display of my image on television came anorexia. I became almost afraid to eat. I wanted desperately to be as thin as Laraine Newman on "Saturday Night Live," but New York streets were filled with things to eat—hot dogs and falafels, pizzas, ice cream, pretzels, charbroiled steak with smells that steamed out of street vendors' stalls. Food was a comfort amidst all the stress in my life.

Around the second year of "Saturday Night Live" I taught myself to throw up. I became bulimic before medical science had even given it that name. I got to be just as thin as I wanted, but the bingeing and purging overwhelmed my life. I was a total professional about my work, but my private life was all obsessive eating and throwing up. I wasn't interested in drugs because I had food. Like any addiction, the eating disorder took charge and left little time for life.

In the three years before my cancer diagnosis, I had begun to change. Through therapy and with Gene's help, I had overcome my eating disorders. I had retaught myself to eat, and left bulimia far behind me. Gene introduced me to people like Mel Brooks and Anne Bancroft and Carl Reiner—people who survived their careers and their successes with good health. I cut down to six cigarettes a day and gave up drinking entirely. I began exercising daily—tennis lessons and swimming. I even stopped chewing gum. I was following a rigorous anticancer diet and even had an apron from the American Cancer Society that had a big chart on it with foods you are supposed to eat and foods you aren't supposed to eat. I thought I could counteract my genetic predisposition to cancer through proper nutrition. I suppose what was happening was that I was beginning to care about my life.

I learned much later that we do things in life that are considered "towards life" and things that are "against life." I filled many years with "against-life" behavior. I was so defiant and so funny that I thought I could smoke and say, "Fuck you—fuck you, cancer." I remember, when someone said to me, "Why do you smoke?," I'd flap back with "At least I have a say in my own death. At least I'm causing it, instead of having it sneak up on me." I could stay up all night and roam the streets of New York looking for food, alone at two or three in the morning, not feeling that there was any danger. Nothing could touch me. I let stress and pressure run my precious life, and then when I caught on and began to change, cancer came along and said, "Remember how you tempted death? Well, here's your opportunity."

I always felt that the point of my comedy was to say what the other person was thinking before he said it so I could catch him off guard. I always thought that my comedy grew from my neurotic way of life—the way that I would think *The plane is going to crash* before it took off, so then it wouldn't ever happen. I never leave the house without thinking the house will blow up or catch fire or whatever, because it's all like a magic way of making it not happen. I thought I was controlling my chances of getting cancer by thinking I might get it and being neurotic and funny about it. But it doesn't work. I realize now that it doesn't work.

There was a time in my life on "Saturday Night Live" when all of life was there only for me to find out what was funny about it. The news never meant anything to us on "SNL" because we always looked at it just to see how to satirize it. Nothing in our personal lives was sacred. We used all of it for material on the show. The most important thing was those ninety minutes live on Saturday night. So what if your whole world was falling apart as long as you could find a joke in it and make up a scene. Millions of Americans saw what we did, and it was a charmed time. We thought we were immortal, at least for five years. But that doesn't exist anymore. Now real stuff happens. Once we did a sketch about cancer and I played a woman being diagnosed as having breast cancer. I thought it was so funny because I carried my purse —actually a big clutch bag—over my chest for the whole scene. I sang a song once called "Goodbye Saccharin." I sang that I had to have saccharin because sugar would make me fat and I'd rather be thin and get cancer than have bulging thighs. It came back to haunt me.

But it *was* a charmed life—until Belushi died. In those five years nobody ever died and nobody ever got horribly sick. Belushi made me laugh like you couldn't imagine. I adored him. He was the one who gave me my first job in New York. In 1974 he called me up in Toronto where I was doing Second City. He was working with "The National Lampoon Radio Hour" and *National Lampoon* magazine because he had done the show *Lemmings* for them in 1973 and it had been a huge success Off-Broadway and then on a national tour. The *Lampoon* people wanted him to do another show, and they were letting him direct it. He could choose the cast. He asked me to be "the girl" in a show that would include himself, Joe Flaherty, Harold Ramis and Brian Doyle-Murray.

In August of 1974, I took a train to New York City to work on the show. It was a very lonely, hard time for me because New York was so big and so weird and I was always wandering around looking for the sky like a country bumpkin. Belushi and his girlfriend, Judy Jacklin (later his wife), looked out for me and all the guys in the cast. They were like the mama and papa. They'd lived in the city the longest and knew the ropes.

Belushi was a mentor to me. We had worked together at Second City so he knew my work. But I think the reason he hired me was that I was a good audience. All the guys liked to have me around because I would laugh at them till I peed in my pants and tears rolled out of my eyes. We worked together for a couple of years creating

The National Lampoon Show, writing "The National Lampoon Radio Hour" and even working on stuff for the magazine. Bill Murray joined the show and Richard Belzer; Dan Aykroyd was around and Christopher Guest and Paul Shaffer. But Belushi was the driving force. *Force* is the right word to use for Belushi. Everything he did was suicidal—the way he ate, the way he drank, even the way he walked and moved. He would throw himself up in the air and splash down on the ground. His characters were suicidal. He was the master of kamikaze comedy. When he died, it didn't seem so strange. But I knew I didn't want to be the second one to go.

It is so hard for us little human beings to accept this deal that we get. It's really crazy, isn't it? We get to live, then we have to die. What we put into every moment is all we have. You can drug yourself to death or you can smoke yourself to death or eat yourself to death, or you can do everything right and be healthy and then get hit by a car. Life is so great, such a neat thing, and yet all during it we have to face death, which can make you nuts and depressed. It's such an act of optimism to get up every day and get through a day and enjoy it and laugh and do all that without thinking about death. What spirit human beings have! It *is* a pretty cheesy deal—all the pleasures of life, and then death. I think some people just can't take the variables; they just can't take the deal—that is why they drink themselves silly or hide away or become afraid of everything. Sometimes I feel like I couldn't take the deal—it was just too much. Cancer brought life and death up close.

What made it all even worse was that I'm a comedienne who does Roseanne Roseannadanna and all this stupid stuff, and then gets the most unfunny thing in the world. It wasn't as if I was a dramatic actress associated with great tragic roles. I kept thinking there must be a purpose to this somewhere. There had to be. How could Gilda Radner, whose name was synonymous with comedy, now become synonymous with cancer? What good is that going to do? How am I going to make cancer funny? How am I going to get people to laugh about it?

I just didn't want to be in tragedy. I didn't want to be tragic even for a moment, not to any nurse who came into my room, not to anyone I knew in the world. I wanted only to be what I am—a comedienne, a jester. Everything was working against me, but I wasn't going to accept that fate. I would be funny again. Each day in the hospital following my operation I just tackled what had to be done. If it meant having the strength to walk around the hospital floor twice or to go in and have surgery to have a Port-A-Cath put in, I ignited my spirit to do it.

A couple of years before I got cancer I read a book called *Disturbances in the Field* by Lynne Sharon Schwartz. I told Gene about it because it was one of the most horrifying and intelligent books I ever read. It was about a woman my age and her circle of friends. She was highly educated, a philosophy major and a musician. She played the piano and lived in New York and married a wonderful man, unlike some of her friends, who had troubled marriages or were in and out of relationships with no sense of continuity. They had four children right away— and she continued to do her music. The children were aged seventeen, fifteen, twelve and ten. One afternoon, the two youngest children were coming home from a skiing trip that they had gone on with their school and their bus was in an accident. The two children were killed. She had explained before that there are "disturbances in the field" when something happens that you don't expect—for instance, this accident—and that changes everything. In one moment she lost her two beautiful youngest children. The book follows her and her husband through their mourning. She remembers that when she was a little girl, her parents had a house on the beach in Cape Cod, a summer place where they took her and her sister when they were about the age of her children who died. They'd go down to the beach and there were always lots of people there, and everybody had umbrellas that looked alike. She and her sister would go and play by the sand dunes, but it was hard to tell where their parents were. So her father began to tie a pair of tennis shoes on one of the spokes of their umbrella so when the two little girls looked over, they could see right away where their parents were. She longed for that time when you could believe your parents were protecting you.

I remember riding in the backseat of my father's car and thinking I was really safe. He would take me to school and I used to play this game where instead of sitting with him in the front, I would ride in the backseat and pretend he was chauffeuring me to school. He could truly protect me then. If my parents were home, I was safe, and things didn't happen—cancer, bus accidents, plane crashes or wars. As long as my parents were home, everything was all right. The woman in the book couldn't change what happened to her children. She couldn't protect them the way her father had when he had tied the shoes to the umbrella so she and her sister could know where their parents were. In the hospital I remembered that book, thinking inside, *Please, someone protect me from this cancer. Make me feel safe again.*

The night before my first chemotherapy, I was lying in bed and Gene walked in the doorway of my hospital room. He was carrying a little pink umbrella with shoes tied to it.

7.

Chemotherapy

When I finally came home from the hospital I felt like the inside of a radio. A head of a Hollywood studio once gave me a radio that you could see the inside of because it was clear plastic and lit with pink neon inside. You could see every intricate wiring detail, hot and exposed. That's how I felt. The toxicity in my body from the chemotherapy made me feel like those swirling geometric patterns and designs of the 1950s—you know, the red vinyl furniture with black pianos on it, and neon lights and chrome watches with geeky things sticking out of them. It felt kind of like a mixture of everything that has come back as nostalgia now—leopard skin and black patent leather with red lightning jags on it, Jimi Hendrix guitars and felt skirts with musical notes and poodles on them, fins and wings on fuchsia Cadillacs, pink and black shoes that are too pointy, Melmac bowls and Max Head-room, neon yellow toreador pants and gold lamé bar stools. That's what chemotherapy felt like in my body when I came home—like there were constant electrical currents from the 1950s running through me.

In the hospital I was told that I was to have nine sessions of chemotherapy spaced approximately three weeks apart and involving two major chemicals, called cisplatin and Cytoxan. The number of treatments had been determined through experimentation that is constantly being revised. With only six sessions there was recurrence of cancer, and with twelve the side effects became too severe. I had my first treatment before I left the hospital. So not only was I coming home as someone recovering from major surgery, but I had just been zapped with chemicals to kill any cancer that was left in my body. That's all the dreaded "chemo" treatment really is: doses of chemicals—drugs, medications—administered intravenously or in shots or in pills that have been found to kill cancer cells. Of course, a lot of healthy cells get knocked around in the process, causing side effects like hair loss, nausea, fatigue and lowered blood counts, but the healthy cells regenerate. The hope is that the cancer cells won't.

There are many different types of cancer—and many different types of cancer cells. Different chemicals are used in various combinations depending on the cells to be attacked. Cancer cells are actually regular cells that are dividing too quickly. These chemicals are toxic to those quickly dividing cells. My electrical feeling was a response to all the medications I had been on since my surgery. Besides the chemotherapy, I was taking painkillers and on top of that my hysterectomy had created hormonal changes.

I came home with the intensive care nurse who had been assigned to give me all my treatments. She would administer my chemo in the hospital for each of the nine sessions. My internist had asked for her to do this and to oversee my case. Her name was Jodi. She was tiny, just about five feet tall, with dark black hair and glasses. She is a skilled and committed nurse and she took on my case with a vigor and devotion that were amazing. She made herself available by phone for Gene and me to talk to at any time. She arranged and coordinated all my doctors' appointments and hospital visits and kept complete records on my progress. The day I came home from the hospital, she leaned down beside my bed and gave me a little program to follow. She told me to try to get out of bed every day—to get dressed and try to write something in a journal. She encouraged me to make plans to accomplish a small task. Each day home, I'd feel a little better. The electrical feeling began to leave my body and the nausea I'd had subsided. I would try not to look in the mirror, but even so I would lie in bed and get flashes of what I looked like. I thought, *This can't be. It can't be happening to me. How could this nightmare be happening?* But every day I would get up and try to go into our pool, even if I could hardly move. Once I got in the water I felt looser, better. Gene paid to keep the backyard pool heated through the winter months. I didn't go in if it was too cold, but we had it so hot that most days it was like a bathtub. I would go from there right into a warm bath. This could take me about three hours because of how frail I was. I'd be dragging myself in and dragging myself out. Then I would sit and write in that journal—sometimes just saying, "I swam, I took a bath, I got dressed today." Then I'd crawl back into bed, breathless and exhausted.

Our friend Grace came from Connecticut to live with us in California, to take care of me and the house so that Gene could keep working on his writing projects. The studio had told him they'd postpone the movie in France until he was available, but after a short time, they went ahead and made it without him. Grace made our bedroom into the most beautiful fantasy place. Gene had bought a new mattress for the bed and she bought new sheets with ruffles on the pillows. She bought a fresh red-and-blue quilt she had found in Connecticut. Grace and Gene bought new curtains and there were always fresh flowers and a sweet breeze. Then Grace got me wonderful books to read—like *Cold Sassy Tree,* about a family in a place called Cold Sassy Tree, Georgia, at the turn of the century. The characters were wonderful, and I loved that book. I lost myself in the novel. The minute I finished that book Grace was there with another. She used to be a librarian. She brought me Betty Rollins's book about her fight with breast cancer. Grace herself had had uterine cancer eight years before so she was my support group. With Gene and Grace and Jodi, I had wonderful love and comfort around me, not to mention Sparkle, chief personal watchdog.

Months later Grace told me that the day I came home from the hospital, she was frightened. When she put me in my bed, she had to help me undress like a baby. I felt so tiny. Afterward Grace went to her room and cried for a half hour. She thought I was going to die. She had never seen me so weak and hollow-looking.

In the meantime, Gene was giving the performance of his life. It was always very important to Gene that he get his sleep, and I was careful not to wake him up in the middle of the night. But when I came home from the hospital, he said. "Anytime you want to get up in the night or you are scared, or afraid about something, just wake me up and we'll have a cheese party." Whenever his dad was in a good mood, he would say, "Let's have a cheese party." It didn't have to be cheese, it could be anything, but Gene's father would call it a cheese party. This should have been a clue. I should have known then that Gene thought I was going to die because he would never have said, "Wake me up in the middle of the night." His performance convinced me. And it happened that I did wake Gene almost every night. I would wake up sweating and out of breath, running from a nightmare that didn't end when I woke up. I would cry in deep moans, wailing like a wounded animal—getting louder and louder to try to drown out what had happened, what I looked like, what could be. Gene held me, rocked me, but he couldn't protect me from the cancer. The night was the scariest time.

In the daytime, lying in bed, I was glad I was in California because there was still green outside the window in November. Sometimes I would just lie in bed, looking out and thinking what a beautiful scene it was, and how much I wanted to be alive. I listened to music. I watched television. I read. And one day, lo and behold, my little ninety-five-pound body started to get hungry. I hadn't really eaten in over a month.

I started to want things from my childhood that I hadn't thought of in years. I wanted French toast. Grace was so happy I was hungry that she made it right away. Suddenly food was all I could think about. I wanted oatmeal and brown sugar. I wanted pancakes with bacon and syrup. I wanted bagels with cream cheese. Somehow as my taste buds came back, they came back for foods of my childhood, things that were in the fridge and the cupboards when I was little—Cameo cookies, Muenster cheese, sour cream. Gene and Grace were always going to the supermarket—I kept coming up with new cravings. It got so Gene and Grace wouldn't mention food around me. Hot dogs—I wanted hot dogs with mustard and relish and everything . . . doughnuts and crispy French fries . . . horrible foods, stuff that you would never eat because it would give you cancer. Everything I wanted was stuff that the American Cancer Society said, "Don't eat this—it will give you cancer." But now the doctors said it was more important that I eat and put on weight than anything. I ate whatever I wanted. It seemed like I couldn't put on a pound. I was just skin and bones on my five-foot-six frame. My first night out, we went to Gene's lawyer's house for Thanksgiving dinner. There was a big crowd and I ate everyone under the table. The next day, they sent me a basket of food delicacies as a joke.

Joanna Bull came to the house once or twice a week and guided me through my relaxation and visualization exercises. My psychiatrist made house calls as well.

Three weeks went by and then it was time for chemo number two. I would have to go into the hospital for two nights. The drugs would be administered intravenously through my Port-A-Cath in the hospital. The Alchemist checked my blood work to determine the amount of the chemicals that he could give me. Cytoxan is given to increase the effectiveness of cisplatin, which is relatively new and a very toxic drug. It can make the patient violently ill so doctors have learned that it is helpful to calm the patient with sleeping medications and steroids to avoid violent reactions. Also, cisplatin can be hard on the kidneys and I had to be hydrated with liquids for eight hours before the actual chemo. The Alchemist wanted the chemo given early in the morning because of some study that shows the cancer cells to be more sluggish at that time. Usually chemotherapy is administered as an outpatient procedure, but cisplatin treatment requires hospitalization.

Gene, Sparkle and I checked into the hospital on a Monday evening at 6:00 P.M., right back into the same burgundy and pink room that I'd left three weeks before. I was scared, but my hospital buddies were glad to see me and distracted me with hugs and gossip. I brought a small bag with a change of underwear, my cosmetics, my glasses and the pink umbrella with the shoes attached. The night nurse hooked me up to bottles of water and minerals that flushed through my system. Gene ate dinner in the room. The gynecologist, who had been at my surgery, came in and did a pelvic exam and answered my list of questions. He is a doctor who treats cancers of the female organs. Gene and doggie went home about 10:30 P.M. I took a sleeping pill and the nurse attached a catheter so I wouldn't have to get up to pee. I tried to do my relaxation exercises, but the catheter was so uncomfortable and I felt irritable. The air conditioner whirled in the vent above the bed and my eyes would not close.

At 6:00 A.M. Tuesday morning, Jodi, my nurse, arrived all fresh and perky on her mission to save my life. She handed me three sleeping pills and antinausea medication. I remember I swallowed them, gave her a hug and then I hugged the night nurse goodbye. I don't remember anything after that except getting the shot of steroids, feeling them hit me like hot, prickly lights going on in my whole body. Then I was sound asleep for the next twelve hours. Jodi dripped the chemo into my Port-A-Cath and kept a close watch on all my vital signs, making sure my kidneys were working and flushing the chemicals through my body. From time to time she flicked my legs around in the air to make sure I urinated. I found out all this later. I didn't remember a thing until 6:00 P.M. when Gene and Sparkle arrived.

Gene put Sparkle on my chest and she gave me a little kiss. Someone brought me some food. I have hardly any memory of those moments. I could barely keep my eyes open but I remember Gene's face and one bite of food. The sleeping pills that I took alter short-term memory. Even if I'd gotten sick from the chemo, I wouldn't remember.

Now, for a person like me who wants to be in control of her life, to give up a whole day and to take pills that made me forget was one of my hardest psychological struggles. I was losing a day on earth. When I came out of it I found people had died, stores had gotten robbed, movies had opened, there was weather—a whole lot had happened that I had missed. That really bothered me. A few minutes after six, I went back to sleep and I slept all the way through till the next morning, Wednesday morning. When I woke up, Jodi was there. I thought about this later—she had gone home and been with her husband and watched TV and read books, taken a bath, brushed her teeth and everything. She had had her life and I had just been asleep—like Sleeping Beauty or Rip van Winkle. I slept thirty-six hours from Monday night till Wednesday morning. All the world was going on and I was asleep. One day while I was sleeping Jackie Gleason died. I didn't know until a month after it happened.

In order to avoid nausea, I was on heavy-duty steroids. I was so wired when I woke on Wednesday morning that I could've come to your house and washed your car, cleaned your yard and cooked dinner. My brain was flicking around, my eyes were darting around, my hands were shaking. I don't know what to call it except wired, as though I'd had a million cups of coffee. It was like I didn't even know who I was—I was somebody like me, some weird person who looked like me and dressed like me. My face was puffy from the steroids, as though somebody had just blown me up like a balloon. But I got up, I had some cereal, I got dressed, I brushed my teeth. I packed my stuff and Jodi took me home in the car. The whole rest of the day, everything was altered: I felt like one of those animated books where you just flip through the pages with your thumb—like the early moving pictures. That is what my life was like. My taste buds were weird. Things tasted weird. I watched a movie on television to make the day go by. I played Scrabble and I won, so something was working in my brain. Somehow that day went by, thanks to Grace, Jodi and Gene. They kept me busy.

By the time evening came around, I wasn't nauseous, I was just tired. I was taking steroids at home. I was to go off them slowly, four Wednesday, three Thursday, two Friday, one Saturday. When I got in bed with Gene Wednesday night, I was glad to be home.

The steroids masked the side effects of the chemotherapy. As long as I was on them, I was able to watch television, do needlepoint, and be fairly peaceful. But eating was very unpleasant. I craved salty things because I could taste them. I ate what I ordinarily wouldn't eat. I wanted cheeseburgers, cheese and pickles. Lettuce and vegetables tasted like plastic. The highly salty, tasty things were good, but bland foods tasted like something they weren't, and that was too strange. It was too weird when a carrot tasted like a ceramic kitchen magnet.

Then, when I couldn't take the steroids anymore, I woke up nauseous and depressed. The nausea was low grade, like what I heard other women say it was like to be pregnant. The depression was due to steroid withdrawal. The nausea lasted Sunday, Monday, Tuesday, Wednesday, and then miraculously it was gone. But those four days were the longest days on earth.

A few mornings later, I woke up and the first thing my eyes focused on was hairs all over my pillowcase. I reached into my punk haircut and a bunch of strands came out in my hand. Looking down onto the bathtub floor while I was shampooing, I saw it was covered with hair swirling toward the drain—my hair. I was devastated. It was like the scene from *Psycho* when Janet Leigh is in the shower—I screamed. I became hysterical the way people do in the movies. Gene and Grace ran in. I felt so vulnerable because I was naked, too. They both said the right thing, "Gilda, it means that the chemo is working. It's not important." My wonderful husband always made me feel that there was nothing unattractive about it or nothing that frightened him even for a second about it. It really was just a few days when it drastically fell out. It happened so fast and it was so messy—thank God for Grace with the Dustbuster on the pillowcase. I'd get up to go to the bathroom and she would come in and get those hairs before I even saw them.

The next night we went out to dinner at a friend's house and a clump of my hair fell in my plate at dinner. It looked disgusting. I was trying to get it out of the plate before the hostess noticed, but it wasn't like one hair, it was a little clump of hair in the poached salmon with the special Dijon sauce. It seemed like an event only Roseanne Roseannadanna could make up—me trying to get this hair off the plate and then trying to figure out what to do with the hair. I didn't want to eat it even though it was my own hair. And my hair is dark so it wasn't hidable, it was just right out there.

So for about five days my hair was falling everywhere. I had just begun to think I looked like Audrey Hepburn when I started to look like Zero Mostel. There were some strands of hair that oddly held on—you know how Zero would comb a huge clump of hair from the side over the top? Well, this miraculous thing happened to me where some hair stayed in the back, some stayed in the front and in between were huge patches of baldness. It wasn't like Yul Brynner. It wasn't clean, it was messy. Why some hair held on like that, I don't know. Once Gene couldn't resist reaching in and pulling out a clump for himself. He just reached into my head because it was so intriguing to think that hair could come out in chunks when you grabbed it.

The most difficult part of the whole chemotherapy for me was losing my hair. The doctors always tell you that you might not lose your hair because some people don't. But I did. Everything that I always thought I would be strong about made me just the biggest weakling in the world. I couldn't stop crying, couldn't stop feeling ugly. I always said the reason I am so funny is that I am not vain. But I was filled with hatred. I hated everyone on television. I hated all the people on TV commercials who shook their heads and looked great. I hated all our friends. I didn't want to go out of the house; I didn't want to go to any dinners or any parties. My eyebrows stayed, but my eyelashes thinned. Within days, I had no body hair, including no pubic hair. It seemed so unfair, not only to have to go through chemotherapy, but to feel marked with baldness like the mark on a house that was quarantined when someone had scarlet fever in the old days.

Gene and I had a woman come in to design a wig for me in this little punk cut, made with real hair. It cost an extraordinary amount of money. When I tried it on I despised it. I wouldn't put it on. I thought it looked like a wig. I was so angry that this was happening to me. Someone came and went shopping for wigs for me. I tried on all these wigs, brown curly ones, blond with bangs, wild Tina Turner styles. I belligerently settled on this little Peter Pan–looking thing—in fact, it was called "the Peter Pan" and it cost five dollars and fifty cents. It was very dopey, and when I wore it out in the light it looked fake and vinyl. I should have left on the tag that proudly screamed, "It's a wig!" It was completely unbelievable. It was a color that no one's hair could be. When

STOCK TURN-IN SLIP

QTY.	PART NO.	DESCRIPTION	MO #		
				COMP	INC
				COMP	INC

← ← ←
CIRCLE ONE

SHIP TO:

INSP. STAMP

DATE _____

LINE RETURN _____

SHOP ORDER NO. _____

TURNED IN BY _____

M101-2/91

I had to go out to my weekly doctors' appointments, Gene or Jodi would drive me, and I'd slump down in the car with a hat or scarf on my head. I'd peer out the window at Los Angeles—at traffic and joggers. I'd feel left out of the world.

Just like I did on "Saturday Night Live," I began to lie in bed before I would go to sleep and try to think up characters. Who could I be to get through this? Friends invited us to a dinner party and I wouldn't go because I couldn't think of who to go as. Let's face it, there aren't many women with no hair. I thought that maybe I could put on a turban and go as Winnie Mandela. Or maybe go as the female Telly Savalas. I worked on it every night lying in bed—then all day long. But if people came to the door, I would hide in the house, ashamed and angry.

At my original surgery there was a nurse who talked to me about how I might lose my hair from chemo. She gave me some paper surgical caps that nurses wear over their hair in surgery. I liked them. I put one on and I thought that it looked kind of cute. So after weeks of me parading around with that almost naked Zero Mostel head, Grace went out and bought fabric. She used the surgical hat as a pattern and made me a whole bunch of caps in different colors. For a while, that is what I wore.

A bit later I began to do a lot of shopping in a store called Laise Adzer in Beverly Hills. It has Moroccan-style women's clothing—lots of cotton with fringe. It also has scarves you can wrap around your head, and turbans are shown with all the clothes. I realized that if I just bought clothes like that and dressed that way, I could wear scarves around my head. That would hide my baldness. I bought a whole bunch of scarves and a couple of outfits that I could wear if I got invited somewhere. I wore the caps Grace had made me and wrapped the long, narrow Laise Adzer scarves around them. The happier I was, the more I piled on my head. I dressed like a harem girl. At last I had found a character in which I could come back into the social world.

I remember the first night we went out to dinner. I had a Laise Adzer coat that looked like Joseph's coat of many colors. My head was piled with colorful scarves. I'd lost lots of eyelashes because of the chemo treatments, so I, who never wore mascara because I hated taking it off, suddenly had to use makeup. Joanna said you have to try harder when you have cancer. It helps to wear makeup because you lose eyelashes and the medications alter your face. I went out and bought makeup and started lining my eyes and putting mascara on the five or six eyelashes I had left on each eye. I looked nice and nobody stared at me like I was weird because I had a whole look, this Laise Adzer look. I was even in style.

Still, even after a lovely dinner, I came home in my new clothes and felt depressed. When I took off my outfit, there was my bald head. I was still a cancer patient. I was different.

Chemo three was scheduled right before Christmas. I had a cold or virus, and I had been having horrible gas pains in my stomach. I went to the Alchemist for the examination before my treatment. He felt my stomach. It was as hard as a rock so he sent me to another office to have X-rays taken. The X-rays showed that I had a partial bowel obstruction, which can happen after extensive surgery. It meant they couldn't do the chemotherapy. The bowel obstruction had to be treated. I was put in the hospital immediately—same room, new procedure.

To treat a partial bowel obstruction without surgery, the doctors tie a rubber bag with mercury in it (because mercury is heavy) to the end of a long, narrow plastic tube. They put the tube and bag through your digestive tract, weighted by the mercury. Over a period of hours, it drops through your whole bowel and opens up the obstruction. This may not be a precise medical explanation of the procedure. All I could think about was getting a bag and tube shoved down my nose. The gynecological oncologist came to the hospital to do the job because he is not only an oncologist but also a surgeon. During my months of chemotherapy he took charge of my pelvic exams and any necessary surgical procedures while the Alchemist did my blood work and took care of my general health.

You can imagine the assault on the body from this tubing weighted with a bag of mercury. It was one thing getting past the nose and the throat, but then suddenly you feel it and your whole body is screaming "Get this out of here!" Your stomach reacts by starting to produce lots of acid. Instead of getting my third chemo, I lay in the hospital bed with this tube in my nose. Here I was— a bald woman with a tube in her nose. I lay in the bed and cried that whole night. I stayed in the hospital three days, not allowed to eat or drink anything. I was fed intravenously. It hurt to swallow, and I had a sinus infection at the same time, so I was sneezing and blowing my nose with the tube in it. Suddenly, my whole life consisted of trying to go as long as I could without swallowing because it hurt so much. How I made it through those days I don't even know. The amazing thing about the human spirit is that when you feel well again, you don't remember those awful things.

Gene came every day. We did everything we could to make time go by—played Scrabble, watched television. I remember sitting in that room blowing my nose and wanting to go home for Christmas. But there was nothing I could do except wait for the bowel obstruction to clear. Then they kept taking X-rays to see if it was clear.

From the beginning of my illness, I fought everyone around me about having X-rays. "Do I really need them?" "Do I have to have two?" "Don't you have my X-ray from the last time?" I was still trying to *not* get cancer in the middle of having it. Then a technician told me that the amount of radiation you get in an X-ray is less than you get flying from New York to Los Angeles. Since Gene and I live on both coasts and fly back and forth, I began to think of my X-rays as flying to New York and back. It eased my mind as they clicked away on the X-ray machine.

On Christmas Eve, Gene and Grace came to the hospital and brought me one of my presents. It was from Gene, a fragile diamond bracelet set in gold. He put it on my wrist and closed the clasp. What a lucky, bald-headed, tube-nosed girl!

By Christmas morning the bowel had cleared. The gynecological oncologist came and started to take the tube out slowly. He had to do it a little bit at a time because it hurt my nose so much. It was so painful bringing the tube up, it was the single worst experience I can remember of the whole illness—the cancer, the operation, even the chemo. He pulled a few inches at a time because the intestine is huge and winding and there was a lot of hose in there. The nurse took over, then the gynecologist came back and he started doing it faster. I was crying. It was horrible. I didn't want to live. Finally it was so painful they gave me a shot of painkillers, which made me nauseous immediately so they had to give me an injection of antinausea medicine right away. I became so drugged that the doctor could pull the last foot of tube all the way out really fast, like quickly pulling a Band-Aid off. Lo and behold, the mercury bag was not at the end of the tube.

It was a little rubber bag, like a condom, filled with mercury. They quickly took another X-ray and they saw that it was in the lower bowel. The bag was inside me. The gynecological oncologist said, "There is no problem."

I said, "Has this happened before?"

But I was so stoned I really didn't care; I was so relieved the pain was over.

"There is no danger, and you'll be fine," said the doctor. He went on to say that I would pass it normally, eventually. He let me go home.

Home was wonderful. There were Christmas presents waiting to be opened. And glory of glories, I could drink clear liquids. Then the next day, full liquids (custard and soups), and then solid food. The cancer patient was overindulged by family and friends. I got too many gifts. After I had opened everything, I had fifteen stuffed bears lining my mantel and one clown doll with a tube in its nose from my hospital nurse, Bonnie.

The next morning, I was lying in bed and I had a little

gas. When I got out of bed, there was a ball of mercury on the bed. A silver ball of mercury lying on the sheets. Very Christmasy.

Have you ever seen mercury out of a thermometer? It rolls and it breaks. Kids used to play with it until doctors found out it was toxic if it got in the bloodsteam. When I tried to pick up this ball of mercury, it split into a million little molecules of mercury, and then fell onto the shag rug on the floor. I was worried about being in the same room with it. I was worried about Sparkle. I called the gynecological oncologist. He started laughing because he couldn't believe this had happened, and then he told me there was nothing to worry about. The next time I had a bowel movement, mercury came out in the toilet. It was so heavy it wouldn't flush down. Then later, out came more mercury. I had gone to two different toilets in the house, so there was mercury in two toilets in the house, and there was mercury in the shag rug. Every time I tried to pick it up, it split into thousands of pieces. I was worried about Sparkle, so I called the poison control number.

I said to the lady at the poison control center, "We broke a thermometer and it's in the shag rug—is it dangerous?"

"No."

"How can you pick it up?"

"Use Scotch tape," she said.

Grace and I spent the next seven hours on the floor, trying to pick up the mercury in the shag rug. Every time I would go through the shag rug I would find more balls of mercury. I tried to get it into one big ball and then finally scoop it onto a piece of Scotch tape and take it to the toilet. Then, we couldn't flush it down the toilet. It was too heavy. Finally Grace and I had to rig up this thing with a paper cup and scooper to scoop the mercury out of the toilet. It was lying right in the bottom of the toilet so we scooped it into the cup. But it would split and we would have to keep doing it again and again. Finally we got it and put it in the garbage bag and threw it away. Later, when I had another bowel movement, the rubber bag came out in my stool with little mercury balls in it. It was quintessential Roseanne Roseannadanna. A wise nurse at the hospital told me later, "Never let a gynecologist put anything in your nose."

8.
The War

When I was little I used to lie in bed at night and think about how glad I was that I was a girl and not a boy 'cause boys had to go into the army. I never wanted to fight in a war; it seemed too scary. Now, here I was, deeply embroiled in the battle of my life—a war against cancer taking place inside my own body. Chemical warfare. My weapons were cisplatin and Cytoxan, and just a few days after the mercury bag episode I was back in the hospital to do battle—chemo number three. My continuing sessions with Joanna Bull taught me that my mind was another powerful weapon. Joanna was my drill sergeant. We met every week to talk about cancer and chemotherapy.

Joanna taught me a wonderful thing to incorporate into my daily visualization: that cancer cells are remarkably stupid. They are just the dumbest things you could imagine. They are like the guys in the foxhole who are supposed to be hiding from the enemy but who stand up and say, "I can't take it any more," and then get shot. When they see the chemo coming they run out and yell, "I'm here, I'm here." Your normal cells get hit by the chemicals and they are jolted, but they aren't stupid— they are smart and they say, "I'll just get myself back together again." That's why chemotherapy works, because of how stupid cancer cells are. I loved imagining them this way instead of giving them any power over my body.

During my recovery from the operation, I would lie on my back on my bed and do a very quick Gilda version of Joanna's relaxation. For twenty minutes or more every morning, I would go from relaxation to visualization and imagery. I would curl my toes and relax them really quick; tense my legs and relax them really quick; tense my stomach and relax it quickly; take my fists and hold them and squeeze them together until they shook with tension and then let them go. Next I squitched up my whole face like you wouldn't believe so that the tip of my nose was white, squitched it up and relaxed it; and then I opened my mouth as wide as I could, opened my eyes as wide as they possibly could be, and then let everything go. I found that after going through that, almost torturing my body into tension and release, my body felt totally relaxed.

From this state of relaxation I would visualize, but my visualizations incorporated improvisation. For example, I saw the word *RELAX* as pillows—huge, overstuffed furniture pillows in the shape of the letters. I would imagine crawling into each letter and finding a place in the letter where I could curl up and feel safe and relaxed. In the *R,* I'd go in the hole at the top of the *R* and get in there, and then I'd crawl off the big pillow *R* and crawl onto the *E,* onto the shelf of the middle part of the *E.* They were capital letters, so I could slip down the *L* and sit on the base of it and then crawl back into the hole in the *A* and stay there for a little while, then sit on the top of the *X.* I would be so happy in that little relaxed pillow, crawling all around in there. When I got tired of doing that, I turned it into an air mattress that floated in the pool on a clear, bright, shiny day. I'd lie on the word *RELAX* in the pool and let the sun warm me. Once again I would feel safe and calm.

Joanna encouraged me in one of our sessions to focus on the area of my cancer, the pelvic region and the peritoneal cavity (where the ovaries are). She suggested that I pour healing light in that area. That worked for me, but then I started to visualize it differently. I have always loved to do the laundry. I don't know why, but there is something about washing a towel and then putting it in the dryer and having it come out all clean and warm and fluffy. I used to love to put my face in a freshly washed towel and smell it and then fold it. It was the idea of taking something dirty and making it clean and new. So I began to see my peritoneal cavity as this pink terry-cloth towel that was just washed. Maybe I got the idea in my mind because the doctor who operated on me had said, "We got her clean." The towel was fresh from the dryer, warm and pink. In my mind I would pick through all the little strands of terry cloth to make sure there weren't any little black dots of cancer. If I saw any, I would pick them out the way you'd remove lint from a towel. I saw the chemotherapy as a detergent going through there, washing and cleaning and getting rid of any dirt in the little pink terry-cloth towel inside me.

I realized that you can choose whatever way you want to visualize the battle going on inside your body. When I told Joanna that I was doing this, she was so happy. She saw that I had found my own way, that I'd discovered the tricks—and treats—of visualization.

As I approached chemo number four, I began to feel quite well physically. I had recuperated from surgery. I was swimming twenty minutes a day and playing doubles tennis on Sundays. It was becoming harder and harder to face those chemo Mondays every third week, and to know I wouldn't feel like myself for ten days afterward. I had seven chemos to go. After that there would be a so-called second-look surgery. They would open me up again and take biopsies to see if there was any cancer left, and if so, where.

But after the third treatment I was beginning to feel the effects of so many powerful chemicals in my body. I couldn't compare it to anything I had ever had before. You do eventually eliminate the chemicals, but I was told the cisplatin stays in your body for up to three months. Half of it is eliminated during the hour in which it is administered, but the other half works its way out over months. Because of this gradual accumulation, I found that after each treatment I was a little bit different. I never knew exactly what to expect. And of course every individual responds to these drugs in slightly different ways.

The oncologists have to tell you the worst possible side effects because they don't want to be sued. So the Alchemist said that I could have permanent hearing loss of high-frequency sounds like a dog whistle—the loss someone in a rock band would get. I could experience numbness at the extremities because cisplatin affects the nervous system. There were a lot of other side effects, too, but since cancer kills you, you don't have much choice.

Joanna and I would spend our weekly sessions attacking the hardships of chemotherapy. Although I faced each chemo treatment with great apprehension, she encouraged me to see them as friends. It wasn't easy. There were Mondays when Gene drove me to the hospital and I was crying the whole way—crying and screaming in the car, begging to get out, wanting to open the car door at a light and run away down the street. Lying in that hospital bed on Monday night knowing that the next morning I was going to be zapped and doused with chemicals, and everything was going to change for ten days, I wanted to scream. I wanted to escape, to sneak out of the hospital, take a plane to Hawaii and disappear. But what would I be running from? I would be running away from being cured.

One night in the hospital, about the fifth treatment, I couldn't fall asleep. I knew what was coming in the morning, and I just lay in bed and started to scream.

"Get me out of here. Let me go. I don't want this."

It was about 2:00 A.M. Bonnie, my nurse, had gone to the pharmacy to get everything ready for the morning. As she was coming back, Bonnie heard somebody screaming in the halls. She thought it was some elderly patient. She couldn't believe it when she got to the room where the screaming was and it was me. She calmed me down, gave me a sleeping pill and sat by my bed. The next morning I had the treatment, just the same as the others.

Joanna helped me to understand that it was okay to get scared, and it was okay to get depressed, and it was okay to cry and scream and mourn my health and get it out of my system. I thought I had to be a brave soldier. I thought I had to withstand this treatment and not break down. But Joanna taught me that it was all right to express my feelings. One of the best things Joanna ever said to me was that after the chemicals have gone into your body to kill the cancer cells, you want to get rid of whatever you don't need. You want to excrete them from your system. "Think of crying as just another way of eliminating the chemicals," Joanna said. "Just think that if you cry and cry buckets of tears, you are getting rid of the chemicals you don't need." I always found that after a really good cry, I felt better about everything. I felt as though I got rid of some toxicity, that I got rid of some of the pain and the mourning.

But during the ten days following chemotherapy, I continued to feel weird, edgy and nauseous. I was bald and blown up from steroids. I felt separated from the rest of the world, like the only survivor of a nuclear holocaust, wandering alone amidst radioactive fallout—which, after all, produced the nauseous sickness I felt after chemotherapy. I think that image came to me because I grew up in the 1950s. When I was in school, people still believed that you could survive nuclear war. In Detroit, on Saturdays at one o'clock, the air-raid siren would go off. If you were in your car, you had to get out and lie down beside the curb or sidewalk. In school, we were supposed to get under our desks and put our heads down with our hands over our heads. I remember there would be one kid in the class who was assigned to go pull down all the window shades. But I heard if you saw the nuclear light, you would go blind, so I always thought, *Oh, please, don't let me have the assignment of pulling down all the shades on the windows.* In one school I went to we all had to go into the hallway and put our heads between our legs.

I remember the dramatizations on television. There would be a nuclear attack, but a little girl would have left her stuffed rabbit outside in the fallout rain. She could not have it back no matter how much she cried. People would survive in horrible anxiety in their fallout shelters. I remember a "Twilight Zone" episode where the survivors fought over who would go into the fallout shelter. I had a girlfriend in school whose family actually built a fallout shelter in their backyard. At a shopping mall near our house there was a model of a fallout shelter that you could buy. Whenever that air-raid siren would go off on Saturday, or a show about nuclear war was on television, or the radio would beep for the Civil Defense announcement, I got nauseous. Something about it gave me nausea —probably because my father had been nauseated while being radiated for his brain tumor and the association was etched in my brain. I hated the fear of war, but I knew I was in a war now. Though I was surrounded with love and support, the war I was fighting often made me feel like I'd been abandoned in nuclear fallout.

During the ten days following chemo, I had tremendous mood swings. I pushed Gene's patience to the limit. By chemo number five, I'd eaten my way up to 135 pounds. I felt bloated and fat. When Jodi, the nurse, could get off work, she'd take me out. She usually worked in the hospital intensive care unit, but she would do private duty for my chemos every three weeks. We'd go to little coffee shops, particularly one on Pico called Pappa Pete's. It's an old-fashioned coffee shop, not fancy or health-oriented or anything. It's like the Greek restaurant in "Saturday Night Live"—you know, "No Coke, Pepsi... cheeseburger, cheeseburger." And that is just what I felt like having—cheeseburgers and Pepsi. I remember Jane Curtin and I used to love those sketches. Belushi would take an order and Dan Aykroyd would really cook the hamburgers. Even though we ordinarily never ordered hamburgers, we thought that in this scene it was okay to have a Pepsi and a cheeseburger and a bag of chips. We'd be so happy eating on television—just two pals next to each other.

Now here I was going through cancer treatment and back in a coffee shop, this time with Jodi. I'd have a grilled cheese sandwich with pickles, and maybe some cake and ice cream, and I'd allow everything because it was curing the nausea. As in pregnancy, the eating made me feel less nauseous. Then we'd walk through malls. I couldn't concentrate to buy anything, so we'd walk up and down. Sometimes we'd go to a movie, which was good. It took my mind off everything. It was important to get out. The chemotherapy altered my looks enough that I had some anonymity. Besides, if you are nauseated enough, no matter who you are, you don't look like yourself. Also, if you don't give off the aura of celebrity or act like someone famous, people don't sense it. If I walked through that mall with a zip in my step, conscious of my persona, I knew people would be coming up to me and asking me for my autograph. But when this nauseous, bloated, spaced-out Martian was going through there with her nurse, nobody ever gave a second look.

Sometimes Jodi and I would sit in the coffee shop for three hours or more, and I would watch people come in. There was such a variety of people. They would order french fries, and meat loaf specials, and cheeseburgers. One man in the afternoon had pancakes with syrup and bacon. Sometimes they came and read. Some stayed the whole afternoon in the coffee shop. The waitresses never made us feel that we had to leave, or that they were in a hurry. Jodi was wonderful, and she knew we didn't have to talk; we could just sit there. As I watched the customers, I'd imagine what their lives were. Why were they there? Where did they live? Did they eat there every day? I loved to see the old women who smoked cigarettes. They'd have their meal and their tea, and then they would get cigarettes out of their purses. Maybe they were fifty years old and just looked really old because they smoked, but I imagined they were eighty years old, and they smoked and survived. I had stopped smoking after my diagnosis.

During the eleven or so days between chemos when I would feel well, life got better. I could drive, and I would get interested in shopping and meeting friends for lunch. I enjoyed reachieving my independence, but there was never enough leave from the war. Once a week I still had to go to the doctor—either the internist or the Alchemist or the gynecological oncologist for a checkup and blood work. Jodi often drove me. She'd write down all my vital signs in a yellow notebook, and all my blood counts and levels and weight. She watched over me like a mother hen.

The chemo lowered my white blood count so I was more susceptible to infections, colds, flus and viruses. I wore woolen scarves and coats in the California sun. But after chemo number five, my blood work began to show that the chemotherapy was working. A test that indicated tumor activity, called a CA-125, was returning to a normal level. My internist's eyes were twinkling. The Alchemist was proud, so I tried to barter with him like the true merchant that I was.

"Get me out of some of those chemos."

He wouldn't let me out. I started complaining to Gene, but Gene told me the truth about how precarious my situation had been. He used the scary word *metastasized*. I was glad that until then I hadn't known the truth. I stopped fighting the Alchemist over the chemos.

These months of recovery were also hard on Gene. My moods swung from here to China, and I had a raging anger at my situation. I felt irritable and isolated and often didn't want to be touched. Our sex life was nil. At night, I would sleep stiffly on my edge of the bed, whimpering and fearful. I can only imagine Gene's loneliness —a loneliness that increased through a sense of helplessness in the situation.

When I turned on the television set, I was angry and jealous of everyone. Unlike most people, I see people I know on TV, my whole peer group, people I grew up with. Every time I turned on the television or opened the newspaper to the entertainment section, I found out about everybody I knew. Meanwhile, what was I doing? I imagined being interviewed on television.

"Gilda, what are you doing now?"

"I'm very busy. I'm battling cancer."

They don't write that on the second page of the *L.A. Times* Calendar section. They say things like, "Woody Allen and Mia Farrow are having a baby." They don't say, "Gilda Radner is having treatment for cancer and Gene Wilder is driving her to the hospital." In *TV Guide* they say, "As Jane Curtin moves into her fourth successful season of 'Kate & Allie'..." They don't say, "Gilda Radner just had her seventh chemotherapy, and we feel she is going to be successful in her war against cancer." I go to the movie theater, and there are coming attractions for Dan Aykroyd in *Dragnet*. There are no coming attractions for *Gilda Radner's Hair Grows Back*.

For a performer like myself, it was a depressing situation to be in. I could only feel envious and jealous of people whose lives were going on. I was the only person who cried hysterically at "The Tracey Ullman Show." Her career was taking off, while mine was stalled. I tried to pretend that Kareem Abdul-Jabbar shaved his head to look like me. One day, I was standing in Bullock's department store. I had bought a skirt and was waiting for the salesperson to take my credit card while the two salesgirls were trying to figure out who this celebrity was who had just come into the store. She used to be on the television show, "Gimme a Break." They were going on and on about it—who was she? They couldn't remember, so I was actually getting in the conversation, trying to help them think of who it was. I said, "Was she a regular on 'Gimme a Break' or a guest on the show?"

No one recognized me at all. I began to introduce myself as, "I used to be Gilda Radner." That was how I felt. I used to be her, but now I was someone else.

Another day I was on an elevator. I used to have to hide on elevators because people would recognize me, but nobody recognized me anymore. A couple got on the elevator. The girl had a full head of this new kind of hair that they have now, where it's so curled and kinked out —huge hair, like my hair used to be. She had on a beige suede outfit with a tight, tight skirt. She had a beautiful body. She looked terrific. She got on the elevator with a man whom she didn't know that well because she said to him, "I want to go to lunch somewhere close where they take American Express."

He was tall and handsome and had on a blue suit with pinstripes in it. He was nervous talking to her. He said something like, "But I don't know if I can give you all the information you need because my contacts aren't as good in Los Angeles as they are on the East Coast."

I knew from that conversation that they didn't know each other that well. When they got off the elevator, I started to follow them. I don't know why except that I was curious. I felt they were attracted to each other. I could feel something electric in the air. I felt like I didn't exist. I was just a total voyeur. I felt that I could follow them and I would never be noticed at all. So I did.

I followed them a couple of blocks to a restaurant, but I didn't go in. I noticed he had a wedding ring on his hand because he kept nervously scratching his head. He kept scratching his head and mumbling things.

I made up a whole story about them. At lunch, maybe they would have a drink, relax and start to talk of having

an affair. I made up a life for them that would go on—
what he would tell his wife, what his life was like and
how he must have been confident with women when he
was younger because he was very handsome, but maybe
he had been married a long time and had lost his touch.
I took it the whole way until I couldn't go any further
with them. To me it was another example of me wanting
to get out of my life. My future was more chemotherapy,
then an operation to see if I had any more cancer.

Before I became a celebrity, I used to follow people,
watch them, listen to conversations. So many of my characters came from that voyeurism. Then becoming famous
took it away. Now cancer was giving it back. I was afraid
that cancer was going to give it back for good, all the way
back to where it used to be. Only this time I would be
left shell-shocked and lonely.

One night I dreamt that I had come to host "Saturday
Night Live." They put me in the green room. I watched
the show on a monitor there. They never got to me. They
went through the whole show and never got to me. At
the end someone whom I didn't even know, she must
have been a production assistant or something, came up
to me and said, "We are so sorry, Gilda, but there just
wasn't time for you."

And I said to her, "Oh, well, could you just have someone take me home? I don't have a way to get home."

The Radner family (Gilda, Henrietta, Herman and Michael) pose for a photographer in Florida in 1949.

My dad and I dancing at my brother's bar mitzvah in October of 1954. I'm eight years old, and my dad is the love of my life.

This is the ten-year-old hefty camp-cowgirl version of Gilda.

By sweet sixteen, I'd already tried every diet in the world.

I graduated from the Liggett School in June of 1964. This picture was in the yearbook.

In 1971, I was earning sixty dollars a week doing panto-mimes for kids in Toronto, Ontario, elementary schools.

Still a clown in 1972 (that's me in the bottom row on the left), but this time in my first profes-sional job—the Toronto com-pany of the musical *Godspell*.

Long before our television careers, Eugene Levy and I improvised at Toronto's Second City.

This is a publicity photo for *The National Lampoon Show*. It was taken in New York in 1974. Harold Ramis and John Belushi are holding me up.

Dibby and I having a nice visit after lunch. She let me try on her new silver-gray wig.

The 1976 Not Ready for Prime Time Players of "Saturday Night Live."

Scavullo photographed me for the cover of *Rolling Stone*. Detroit girl makes good.

BOB GEDDES PRESENTS

GILDA
RADNER
LIVE
FROM
NEW YORK
WITH
GUIDO SARDUCCI
AND
ROUGE

Winter Garden

I had always dreamed of being on Broadway. In 1979, I was dancing across the Winter Garden Theatre's billboard—as long as a whole city block.

The company of *Gilda Live* including Paul Shaffer, Don Novello, and G.E. Smith.

Gilda look-alike

Finalists in a recent "Gilda Live" look-alike contest pose inside the UA Cine I theater in Dallas. Over 500 fans flocked to the theater and judged Tami White (far right) the winner for her impersonation of "Lisa Loopner."

Gene and I in *Hanky Panky*. Enemy agents are after us as we plan our escape through the desert. All I care about is whether Gene likes me.

On September 18, 1984, Gene and I were married in the south of France. (Photo by Ralph Gatti)

Sparkle.

Our first Christmas card at home in our Los Angeles four-poster bed.

Magnificent Grace (in Connecticut) holding you-know-who.

After two chemotherapies, I compare heads with my best friend Judy's three-month-old son, Alexander.

The Wellness Community, 1235 Fifth Street, Santa Monica, California 90401, 1-800-PRO-HOPE

Joanna Bull (executive director), Harold Benjamin (founder), and Flo Porter (community coordinator) of The Wellness Community.

A potluck dinner at The Wellness Community. I'm sharing ovarian cancer experiences with my friend Ethel. That guy on the left is my husband.

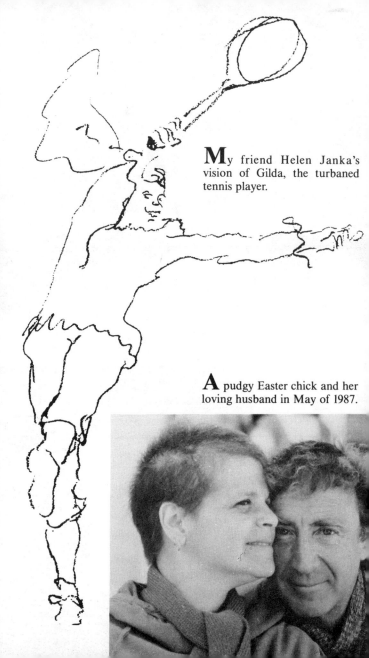

My friend Helen Janka's vision of Gilda, the turbaned tennis player.

A pudgy Easter chick and her loving husband in May of 1987.

Friends for over thirty years—that's Pam on the left, Judy in the middle—relaxing in Connecticut.

In September 1987, we spent two beautiful weeks in the south of France.

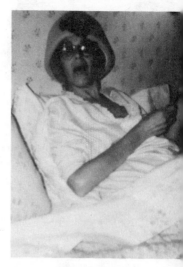

Gilda caught in her glamorous ice-pack getting chemo at home in Connecticut—summer of 1988.

Our Christmas card, 1988.

Cheers!

from the Wilders

9.

The Wellness Community

At one of our regular weekly sessions at my house, Joanna was listening to me drone on about my feelings of isolation, my anger, my hair loss, when she suddenly said, "Everything you're saying I've heard before."

"Am I boring you?" I said defensively.

"No, I just want you to know you are not alone, that other people are going through this. I wish you could have been at this meeting the other night at The Wellness Community. There was a bunch of ladies with no hair, and they were talking about it, talking about how they would take off their wigs and take off their scarves and walk proudly on the beach in Santa Monica, brave warriors battling cancer. I wish you could have been there."

Joanna had brought me literature on The Wellness Community, where she worked, and their newsletter, so

I had read about their activities. They have something they call joke fests—meetings where everyone comes with a joke, just because they know laughing is good for you. I read everything she brought me. But I was afraid to be around people who had cancer, I guess because I wanted to pretend that I didn't have it. And I didn't want to get depressed, more depressed than I already was, something that I was sure would happen if I went to The Wellness Community. I was in conflict about this for a couple of months. Even Grace and Gene said, "Maybe you shouldn't go. Why upset yourself? We know how emotional you are and how you sponge up other people's problems—you probably shouldn't go."

Even my psychiatrist said, "You probably shouldn't go. You probably will get upset."

But I was curious. Every time I saw Joanna I'd ask her about The Wellness Community. What were the events that week? What did it look like? Where exactly was it in Santa Monica? Where do you park? Do you need quarters for the meters? Joanna was encouraging me to come to a sharing group that met every Friday between 11:00 A.M. and 1:00 P.M. Anyone could come on a drop-in basis to share their present experiences with cancer and hear what The Wellness Community had to offer.

In January 1987, after I was over the nausea days of chemo number three, I asked Jodi if she would drive me to The Wellness Community. It was about a half hour from my house. I was so nervous that I would park in the wrong place or I wouldn't be able to find the building or I would be late. I think what I was really nervous about was what this community of cancer patients would be. Jodi and I found the parking lot easily. We were a half hour early, but we went inside. We were the first ones there.

It was a cute little yellow house with a plaque on the front that said, "The Wellness Community." We walked into what looked like a living room in anybody's home. There were two women there with pink sweatshirts on that said "The Wellness Community" and big buttons that said "VICTOR" on them. There was a sweet woman named Joyce who gave us flyers and information and made us comfortable. There were three couches and a rug on the floor and phones ringing in other rooms. There was the cozy smell of food because lunch was being made for us in the kitchen. The chairs were set up in a circle in the main room. Jodi and I sat down, and on a clipboard I signed my name and address and phone number. The form asked what kind of cancer you had or whether you were there as a support person or family member. I wrote my name in an absolutely unreadable scrawling handwriting—and under "Type of Cancer" I printed neatly, "Ovarian."

At about quarter to eleven more people started to come in—all different types of people. They were mostly couples, young and old mixed together. You didn't know who had cancer and who didn't. There was a woman and her daughter. The woman was recently out of surgery and the eighteen-year-old daughter was holding her mother as if she was a little girl. This was their first time at The Wellness Community too. There were lots of women, more women than men. Most of the men came by themselves. One was a real dapper-looking guy in a maroon sport coat and gray pants. There wasn't the feeling that these were sick people, just a lot of different kinds of people, all different socioeconomic levels and ages.

At about ten after eleven the room was pretty much filled with maybe forty people. The two group leaders, Flo and Betty, both eleven-year survivors of cancer (Betty of an advanced case of lymphoma and Flo of a double mastectomy), told their stories of cancer. They explained what The Wellness Community was and what it had to offer every person there. Amazingly, everything was free. There were group therapy sessions that met for two hours a week, available at many different times during the week, called "participant groups." These groups were the only Wellness Community activities that required a commitment. They were facilitated by licensed therapists. Everything else was on a drop-in basis, including instruction in guided imagery and visualization and relaxation three nights a week (like what I had learned from Joanna). There were group sessions for spouses or family members of cancer patients, nutrition and cooking discussions, lectures by doctors—oncologists and psychiatrists—workshops on anger management, potluck dinners and parties, therapy through painting, vocalizing, improvising—all techniques that would help in stress management and improve the quality of someone's life.

I learned why people go to AA meetings or Overeaters Anonymous or other self-help groups, and love them and say, "I have to get back there." If indeed God created the world and then left us on our own to work things out, then getting together with other people to communicate is what we should be doing. I learned at The Wellness Community that that is the most magic thing we have, our ability to open our mouths and communicate with each other.

There was a beautiful woman at the meeting, dressed perfectly in fashion. She said she had breast cancer that had metastasized and was now in her lung and liver, and she was facing a difficult prognosis and a lot of treatments. She was angry and frightened, and she cried. Everyone in the room cried. Then people started to yell advice from their own experience. They told her what had happened to them, how they had had the same prognosis and turned it around through a particular kind of therapy. They traded information. Have you seen this doctor, or tried this hospital? What was happening in the group was that everyone was saying, *"Don't give up."* One man stood up and said that he had had a cancer that had begun with a huge tumor in his stomach. The doctors didn't want to operate on it because they felt he was terminal. He had one doctor who said, "Let's do it anyway." They did, and then he had to have many radiation treatments. His parents told him to be positive and to visualize being well. He was told by his doctors he had maybe two or three months because his cancer was so advanced. Then he said, "That was thirty years ago."

A chill went up my spine.

Betty, one of the group leaders, said that if the statistics say that only eight percent survive a particular cancer, nobody knows who the eight percent are. "Every one of us has just as much right to be in that eight percent as anybody else. If you have cancer," she said, "do everything possible to fight it—do any activity, any event, but participate in your recovery." She was given only a twenty-percent chance—eleven years before. It seemed like the room began to stir with hope.

About forty-five minutes into the meeting, Dr. Harold Benjamin appeared in the doorway. He is the founder and director of The Wellness Community. He is a Beverly Hills lawyer who started The Community with $250,000 of his own money in order to help cancer patients. He had always been interested in the dynamics of group therapy and had a five-year involvement as a "square" (non–drug user) in the controversial Synanon drug rehabilitation program. His wife is a long-term survivor of breast cancer and a sharing group leader active in The Wellness Community. He has written a book called *From Victim to Victor* that explains his philosophy about health, the principles of The Wellness Community. Harold is very charismatic. When he speaks, he does it with great humor and honesty.

"The Wellness Community is not a place to come to learn to cope with having cancer or to die from it. It is a place to learn to participate in your fight for recovery along with your physician. We feel that if you participate in your fight for recovery, you will improve the quality of your life and just may enhance the possibility of your recovery. Your first line of defense against cancer is your own immune system. Scientific studies have shown that depression weakens the immune system—we are here to teach you the tools for the pursuit of happiness so you can be an active participant instead of a hopeless, helpless passive victim. . . .

"Please use us in any way you need and I hope everything turns out exactly as you would want."

He flaps his arms at us not to applaud, but it is difficult

not to be impressed with his ideas and his passion about them.

One of my favorite people at The Wellness Community was a man named Jack. He is eighty-five years old. He says he comes to The Wellness Community every Friday for an "emotional injection." He has his story down like a vaudeville routine. I adored him immediately because his jokes were right on the money and he always got his laugh. He had spinal cancer at eighty-three and was told he would never walk again. He was on chemotherapy in pill form when I met him. He retaught himself how to walk with a walker, and then threw it away. He had a cane and threw that away. He says the only thing wrong now is he can't dance like he used to. He said to his doctors, "With the chemotherapy, how come I lost my hair?"

What he didn't tell his doctors was that he lost it fifty years ago. His wife, Sarah, is there with him. She helps if he forgets any of the jokes.

The first time I had to speak I was so nervous that I couldn't believe it. I didn't say my name, I just very quietly told about my cancer; I said that I was in treatment, that I had had some of my treatments already and that it was very difficult. I had a turban on my head. I thought I looked like an exotic African princess, but I was told later I looked more like Yasir Arafat. I was very shy and quiet about myself. But when other people talked and I saw their spirits falling low, I would yell something from across the room. Someone else would be on cisplatin and I would say, "I am on cisplatin, too. The side effects are rough, but six years ago when they didn't have it, we wouldn't have had any hope at all. Now we do!"

At the end of the two-hour meeting, which went by like a dream to me, I was just invigorated. I was so excited I couldn't wait to go back. I saw the beautiful woman stop crying and help someone else. I saw hope come into people's eyes. I couldn't shut up about it. I talked to Jodi the whole way home in the car. Gene was so worried that I would get depressed and instead I ended up driving everybody else crazy because I told every story that I heard there and how it inspired me and how I couldn't wait to go back there again and how I wanted to lead the group and run the whole thing and I knew this was a great thing and I was onto something wonderful. Joanna kept saying, "Just relax. You can't *run* the thing, you *can't.* You are working on your own recovery. Just enjoy what you are able to do and how you can be helped by it."

Every Friday that I felt well I went back to the sharing group. That was my first step. For the first three times I never said my name or anything, and then one day I opened up and said, "My name is Gilda Radner and I am a performer by trade. When I got cancer it appeared on the cover of the *National Enquirer*. They said, 'Gilda Radner in Life-Death Struggle,' and ever since then everybody has thought I was dead. Well, I'm not dead—cancer doesn't have to mean you die."

Everyone in the room was looking at me a little more closely. It was as though at that moment I became Gilda Radner. I got very funny as I told stories about going to a restaurant and seeing someone back up against the wall because he was so frightened to see me. "I don't know if he was upset because I was alive or because he didn't send me a card."

Suddenly, not only did I have the room laughing, but I felt my thumb going up into the air like Roseanne Roseannadanna. There I was at The Wellness Community, and I was getting laughs about cancer and I was loving it. At the end of the meeting a lot of the women came up to me asking questons like "What kind of chemo are you on?" "What happened when your hair fell out?" And I saw they were looking to me for answers or leadership. I tried to help and say what I felt. Then one of the women also said that she was a comedy writer and she had some material and would I read it—a three-hundred-page screenplay. But another woman who was there said, "Hey, look what she is going through right now—this maybe isn't the right time to bring that up."

The woman who wanted to give me the material understood. It was wonderful because this other woman protected me, and I realized you just have to speak up and say, "Don't cross this boundary." What happened in subsequent weeks was some kind of strange balance about being funny, being Gilda Radner, and being someone going through cancer. I found a way to tell my cancer story and get laughs from it. They started to use me for balance at the meetings after someone had told something really sad. They'd say, "Gilda, would you like to speak?"

Jack or I would come in to lift the room back up. I love to make people laugh, and at The Wellness Community I'd found my role again. It didn't matter there that I was Gilda Radner. It wasn't my reputation. It was who I was and who I always have been—someone who is funny.

You know that joke about the optimist who says, "If the house is full of shit there must be a pony somewhere"? Sometimes when I was wandering around and I was so nauseous I thought, *With all this nausea there must be a baby somewhere.* Then I realized at The Wellness Community that *I* was the baby who came out of this. Even in this form—no hair, kinda puffed out—this little person gets born again. I got my life again. I decided that I had nausea because I was giving birth to myself.

One Friday I was sitting very anonymously in a chair and there was a young man who got up to speak. From across the room he looked very ill. He looked as if he was going through a lot, but when he spoke his whole demeanor changed. He had a very powerful voice. Sometimes people talk and you can hardly hear them they talk so softly, but his voice resonated through the room.

He had a neck cancer, many tumors in his neck, and he was undergoing radiation therapy. He had lost all his taste buds from the therapy and had other complications, but his spirit was amazing. He said the doctors told him he would have his taste buds back in two months, and when they came back he had thirty-six dinner invitations. As he went on, it became clearer that he was a performer. Then all of a sudden he said, "One time I was working in a show in Los Angeles in a small theater in a shopping mall and that lady across the room"—I saw he was looking at me—"you, Gilda, came backstage and threw your arms around me and said, 'I have always had a crush on you—I saw you in *West Side Story* and I have had a crush on you my whole life,' and she made me feel so good."

Suddenly, I looked at him and realized who he was, because I did see the movie *West Side Story* eight times when I was a kid, and there was one of the Jets, Ice, whom I loved to watch dance. His name was Tucker Smith. I saw him again in a little show of Gershwin songs

Gene and I went to. It was a wonderful show, and I did go backstage and hug him and have a crush on him. Now here we were at The Wellness Community sitting across from each other, both battling cancer. There was some balance in the universe in this strange way. When he finished his speech I yelled across the room, "Make that thirty-seven dinner invitations!"

At another meeting we sat together. His spirit was so amazing as he talked about the ways he found to eat to overcome the weight-loss problem, which is a major side effect of radiation therapy because you lose strength. As a dancer Tucker understood that. He found ways to get food down, preparing soups and using a straw. He even found ways of getting noodles through the straw. It was very important to him not to lose weight so he could come through his illness. His will to fight was an inspiration to me.

There was another day when somebody, before he spoke, said "Hi, Gilda" to me. He turned out to be a young man whom I went to camp with when I was fifteen. It was a shock, but this kind of thing caused an overwhelming change in me. I stopped sitting at home saying "Why me?" or being depressed thinking I was the only one. I began to crawl to The Wellness Community like someone in search of an oasis in the desert. My car couldn't get me there fast enough. I couldn't walk fast enough from the parking lot. I couldn't get inside fast enough to be nourished by other cancer patients, and to know I was not alone. I could hire people to be around me, I could pay groups of people to come and go through this with me, but I could never buy what I got there, not ever.

A story that one woman told at The Community had a deep effect on me. She was diagnosed with a particular kind of lymphoma. She immediately went everywhere for every possible cure other than the recognized medical one. She went to Mexico. She went to Europe. She did all the spiritual, mystical cures. She spent thousands and thousands of dollars traveling, looking for an answer. After a year of doing this she had some side effects from experimental treatment that were even worse than her cancer. They drove her back to her medical doctor, and he put her on chemotherapy. She had to take these big pills—some types of chemotherapy involve taking pills. She took these big pills and started to feel better, and her lymphoma was under control. Now she says before she takes the pills each day, she kisses them. She kisses each pill before she swallows it.

When I heard her speak it was a week when I was hating chemotherapy, and she inspired me. She knew chemo was her friend, saving her life, giving her life. My next treatment, when I felt, *Ooh, I hate this, I want to run away, let me get out this,* I just thought of all those faces at The Wellness Community. People who have become friends, all at different stages of cancer, all fighting, all different, some with hair, some with clumps of hair, some with radiation burns—how brave we all are together. I just felt them all around me and it made me be braver. The same way people in gangs can do things that the individual could never do alone, the gang of us fighting cancer makes us all stronger. Sometimes I imagine all their little faces inside my body shaking their fists at the sky, rallying against our common enemy—cancer.

I began to face my treatments and my doctors with a

different attitude. I wanted to know more about my disease and my treatment. My doctors learned to sit still for my long list of questions, and I became an expert on my own case. I started to regain control in my life, to take charge and not be a victim of my situation.

I became more confident in the well world, too. I knew that part of my recovery was to reestablish myself in my regular life, too, like going out with girlfriends and going shopping, playing tennis, going to dinner parties with friends. I was so mad at healthy people for so long that I really felt hateful toward them. Part of my recovery was learning to function in the healthy world. The Wellness Community made that easier too. I felt as though I belonged to a private club, with a very steep admission.

Grace had told me, "It's not *what* happens in life . . . it's how you handle it." The Wellness Community gave me the ability to start handling it. I am a fighter and I started to take action. I wanted to inject my recovery—the doctors, the treatments—with the Gilda spirit, with my humor, my silliness.

One of the first problems I tackled was the business of being asleep for thirty-six hours during my chemo while the world was going on. How could I make facing that out-of-control time more bearable? I had an idea. I had Gene make a videotape of me playing tennis on a Sunday. Just me. You don't see who I am playing with. I keep hitting the ball, and I am not a very good tennis player, but I am running around, jumping around and clicking my heels. We put jokes in it. At one point, instead of a tennis ball, a basketball comes across the net. Sparkle comes out and runs around in a circle and I chase her and then you see all our friends whom we play tennis with applauding me and doing testimonials about how well I am doing. Then I come up to the camera and say, "Through the miracle of chemotherapy, I am able to play tennis as badly now as I did before I had cancer."

Then I name all the chemicals I am on and say, "Look what they have done for my game."

And then I go back and hit more balls. I am wearing my turban on my head, showing all this energy. My plan was to play the videotape in my room while I was asleep. The chemicals would drift into my system to cure me of cancer, and at the same time there would be a tape of me playing tennis. Conceptual art! I was so proud of the idea, and it was another way for me to control the situation. It was the first time I looked forward to chemo, knowing my creative self would be involved.

Gene made the tape, but he forgot to put the sound on. It was just as well because it might have woken me up. So, during chemo number seven, Jodi played that tape for everybody who came in—the internist, the gynecological oncologist, every doctor that came in. They couldn't believe it. It was funny even with no sound. It was Chaplinesque. They really enjoyed it. The Alchemist wanted that tape more than anything. How many times does humor come into the business of oncology and chemotherapy? Every time I went to see him I told him he could have the tape if he would let me out of one chemotherapy. But he wouldn't, thank God.

I started to make plans for each chemo instead of just waiting and dreading the day. I set out to accomplish things. In the days when I was recuperating, Gene was the best customer at the video store. I made it a point to watch every situation comedy to study the form for my future. I did needlepoints and pastel drawings. I wrote, I swam, I made plans before a chemo that I could look forward to after. The day before I went in for my chemo, I would drop off shoes to be repaired and plan to pick them up after—another way of controlling, saying, "I am still alive, I am still functioning." My friends planned dinner parties for the first day I felt better. That is one of the premises of The Wellness Community—even though you are being treated for cancer, your life still goes on. You can still have life, and not only life, but a quality life.

After I'd been going to The Wellness Community for about two months, Gene and I went to a Friday-night potluck dinner. We brought Chinese chicken salad. The same room where the sharing group meets was filled with people and food. There were lots of husbands there with their wives going through cancer and vice versa. I have never been at such a good party. Usually you go to a party and there are judgments going on. You feel judged—people look at what you are wearing or they move away from you if they don't think you are interesting, or they all are looking for someone or something. But a party at The Wellness Community is about celebrating every glorious day of life. Joanna's son was there with a synthesizer and he was playing old tunes from the thirties and forties and everybody was singing and dancing along with him. The voice teacher had us all, about 120 people, make a noise one at a time, till all our noises blended in one huge noise of all different pitches and tones, and we felt held in the hum of the noise.

My friend Helen was there with her eleven-year-old son. She is a single parent who teaches third grade in Santa Monica and is a painter. She had melanoma and is in the middle of radiation therapy. Her son wouldn't eat any of the food there because he thought it would give him cancer. I said, "My husband's here and he doesn't have cancer and he is going to eat."

During the party I watched this little boy. It was the first time he had been at The Wellness Community. He was hating it and thinking it was awful, which I am sure is the way he felt about his mother's cancer. By the end of the evening, he was playing ball on the front lawn with other kids and laughing. When I asked him, "What do you think of the party now?" he said, "It's not so bad."

My friend Linda was there with her two children. She has breast cancer which has metastasized to the bone and she has been in and out of treatment for four years. She is very active in The Wellness Community, especially in activities involving parenting and cancer. She is a beautiful woman, funny and creative. We linked arms and sang every song at the top of our lungs.

By coincidence, I met another woman at the party exactly my age, who had the same operation I had, two weeks before me. While in the hospital recuperating from her surgery, she saw the *Enquirer* article about me and wrote me a letter. She never mailed it because she didn't know where to send it to, but it said she was going through the same thing. She is a schoolteacher. She was one treatment ahead of me and we couldn't stop talking to each other about everything. "How did this happen?" "What was your blood count on that?" "When is your second-look operation?" She had a scarf on, not a wig, and I kept wanting to just kiss her head because she had the same amount of hair I had—*none*. It was like going to a party when you were a teenager and meeting someone you had so much in common with that you just couldn't believe it. That night when we got home from the party, my head was swimming trying to relive the moments of it. It was like falling in love. Gene was invigorated seeing cancer patients dancing and singing and laughing and celebrating life.

To this day I have the highest regard for the work of The Wellness Community. I wish there were a thousand more of them. There is nothing woo-woo or mystical or weird about The Wellness Community. The concept is simple and honest. I often said to Joanna or Gene that it reminded me of the early days of "Saturday Night Live" when we had our innocence and we believed in making comedy and making each other laugh. We were just working together to entertain, like kids playing together. The Wellness Community has that same naïveté and honesty. Its sole purpose is to provide a community for people who have cancer to come and play in, to make their lives better, to have an opportunity to help themselves and to help other people.

The hardest part of committing myself to The Wellness Community and becoming friends with people was learning later that someone who had become close had died. The course of cancer isn't always what we hope. I was learning that death is part of life. But if I hadn't gone to The Wellness Community, think of all the love I would have missed. While we have the gift of life, it seems to me the only tragedy is to allow part of us to die— whether it is our spirit, our creativity or our glorious uniqueness.

10.
The Comedienne

I grew up in Detroit, but my mother couldn't take the winters so every November my family would go to Miami Beach and live for maybe four months, and then come back to Detroit. During those four months in Florida, my father traveled back and forth to oversee his hotel business. I would start school in Detroit in September, and by November my parents would take me out of school and take me to Florida where I would attend school for November, December, January, February and part of March. Then we would go back to Detroit and they'd put me back in my school there until the summer. This went on all the way through fourth grade. I couldn't get attached anywhere, and the same thing happened to my brother. I can remember waiting behind the door to go into a classroom in the middle of March where all the kids had been together the whole year. They would think a new girl was coming and it would be me, that same old girl from September. I didn't have any friends. I was a big risk as a friend. Who would want to be friends with someone who wasn't going to be there half the time?

My birthday parties were desperate. There were never any school friends to invite. I always had to have my relatives. My brother has some film of all my birthday parties starting from one year old. It's so sad because every birthday party has the same relatives—all a year older. In Florida there was one girl in my class I kind of made friends with. I invited her over to my house for dinner. During dinner I had a crying tantrum over something that I can no longer remember. It must have been a huge thing or I wouldn't have done it in front of this potential friend. The next day there was a "show and tell" time and she stood up and told the whole class how she went to my house and I had a temper tantrum at dinner. It was horrible.

My brother and I ate ourselves into little balloon children. We looked like no-neck monsters. I was just a mediocre kid. My parents sent me to summer camp every year and every year I was scapegoated. It wasn't so much what the other girls would call me, but they wouldn't let me play with them. In "the princess game" there would be controlling girls and pretty girls. The controlling girls would make a pretty girl the princess and the controlling girls would be advisers to the princess. The fat girl would be the servant or something, and that would be me. At night, I'd be in my bunk sneak-eating Tootsie Roll Pops and pistachio nuts that my mom had sent me and thinking about how to belong. I couldn't be as pretty as the pretty girls and I couldn't be as controlling as the controlling girls. It wasn't in me.

My father was very funny. He loved jokes and he loved life and he had great spirit. He would do silly jokes like, "Don't suck your thumb because it's got a nail in it." He thought that was the funniest joke he had ever heard. He was corny and he loved to watch me perform. He called me his "little ham." My mother has a great sense of humor. She isn't consciously funny, but almost the only thing that gets through to her is to make her laugh. She has an infectious response to humor so it was a way of getting to her when nothing else worked.

My parents put an ad in the paper for a live-in nurse, or nanny, when I was four months old, and Dibby came. Her real name was Mrs. Elizabeth Clementine Gillies, and she was from Canada but she was visiting her cousins in Detroit when she saw the ad. After she met my parents, they took her upstairs to see "the baby." She says that I was lying on my stomach in my crib and I turned my head on the side and smiled at her and I won her heart. My parents hired her right away. My mother insisted that she wear a white uniform, white hose, and white shoes. She bought those that day and came back the next day and stayed for eighteen years with our family. She was in her early fifties and had been a widow since after World War I. She had raised three children of her own, and now was starting a whole new life. When I learned to talk, I couldn't say Mrs. Gillies so I called her Mita Dibby, then just Dibby.

Dibby and I became inseparable. I owe a lot of my humor to her. When I would come home crying because someone called me fat at school, she would tell me, "Say you're fat before they can. Let them know that you are fat and you don't care. If they say you are, just make a joke about it and laugh. Just you tell them before they get to it." She coached me through my teens, and humor became my tool for handling life.

Dibby is the person I modeled Emily Litella after on "Saturday Night Live." Emily Litella was the spunky editorialist on "Weekend Update" who got everything wrong but was emphatic about it until she found out she had misheard. "Never mind," Emily Litella's famous response, is straight from Dibby's mouth.

Dibby turned ninety-six years old in March of 1989. Last week she told me on the telephone (we speak every week), "I can't hear and I can't see and I can't walk, but other than that I'm fine."

I grew up in the midst of that indomitable spirit.

When I was ten years old, I asked my parents if I could go to a private school. The girl who lived across the street went to an all-girl private school on the east side of Detroit, and she liked it. I remember going like an adult to negotiate with my parents about wanting to go to this private girls' school. Of course it cost a lot of money to go there, and I think I told my parents that I thought I would get a better education. They agreed to it. By this time, my brother was in high school and it was becoming more difficult to take us in and out of school.

I loved the Liggett School for Girls. I loved my fifth- and sixth-grade teacher, Miss Cole. She had a thick Irish accent and she was the best teacher there could ever be because she rewarded academic excellence with creativity. It was a wonderful plan. If you did well in mathematics, you were allowed to be in Miss Cole's oil-painting class. And if you did well in geography, you could be in her dancing class. She taught us girls how to ballroom dance. I still lead now because of her class. If you did well in general, you could be in the plays that she wrote. She was rewarding me with the things that I loved the most, so I started to do well. I went from being a mediocre student to being a good student. Today I can't remember half the things I learned in my life in school, but I remember what Miss Cole taught.

I stayed at Liggett from fifth grade to my high school graduation except for my junior year in Mumford High School, the school Eddie Murphy went to. I wanted to meet guys that year; I felt confined in an all-girls school. But in senior year I went back to graduate from Liggett because I missed my friends and the school's traditions. I had found myself there. My personality was formed there. I became an excellent student in high school. I sang alto in a double quartet (two girls on each part, singing in harmony), I was on the dramatics board and I worked on every play that got done. When I was a senior, I directed a very serious mystery called *Anti-clockwise*. It was a drama but the audience started to giggle halfway through and continued laughing till the end. I didn't go to school for two days afterward.

I enjoyed performing at Liggett. In *The Mouse That Roared* I played Tully Bascombe, the male lead. I always got the male parts because I had a strong voice. When we actually gave the performance after rehearsing for weeks and weeks, somebody spoke the wrong line in the first act and skipped to the second act, and we finished the play really fast. As a result most of my part was cut, but everyone said I was great—and the loudest one. During my Liggett years, I found out that I was funny. Humor became the foundation of my life. But if humor was the foundation, men were definitely the first floor.

To a great extent my life has been controlled by the men I loved. I don't think I am ambitious. My biggest motivation has always been love. I would see a guy that I would fall in love with and then I would just want to be with him and go wherever he went. I'd go until I didn't want to be with him anymore or he didn't want me. Then I would see someone else and go wherever he went and do what he did. I have always found men who were funny, irresistible. It's rare that I ever based love on looks or superficial things, but if a guy made me laugh—and that didn't mean he had to be in comedy professionally —I was hooked.

After graduating from Liggett, I spent six years at the University of Michigan as an undergraduate majoring in public speaking and oral interpretation—six years because I dropped out whenever the opportunity presented itself. Sophomore year I went on a date and stayed out all night. Rules were strict in 1965. I got in so much trouble that the dorm board said I'd have to stay in every weekend for that school year. So I dropped out that semester and returned in the summer. I never took a full load of courses and I spent hours in the dean's office convincing him that there was too much pressure for me academically. What a mouth I've always had. In the meantime, I was very active in the Theater Department and began to make a name for myself. I had comic roles in University of Michigan productions of *Lysistrata, Hotel Paradiso* and *Camelot.* My photograph was in the window of the five-and-ten-cents store downtown advertising the opening of the Ann Arbor Civic Theatre's production of *She Stoops to Conquer.* I thought I'd stay in Ann Arbor forever, an eternal undergraduate. I almost did.

In 1969, while National Guardsmen lined the streets of Ann Arbor and the air was filled with pepper gas, young people were moving to Canada, angry over American political policies and resisting the draft. I moved too, but because I fell in love with a Canadian sculptor and wanted to be his wife and a homemaker. I have always had this fantasy that I would live on a farm and wear a print dress and have lots of kids and animals and a life filled with hard work feeding the kids and animals. I would farm the land and at night sit on the porch in the print dress with my husband and watch neighbors walk by and traffic go by. To pursue this fantasy, I left my burgeoning career in Ann Arbor Civic Theatre and moved to Canada. I never graduated from the University of Michigan. Years later they put Roseanne Roseannadanna on the cover of the alumni bulletin, so I figure Roseanne graduated for me.

In Toronto, Canada, I began my professional career. My homemaking fantasy and my romance lasted about a year and four months. We never got to the getting married part. There was no farm or children or print dresses. I learned to cook and helped him with his art shows, but I sublimated my performing ego and became very depressed. I went to night school at the University of Toronto and University of Wisconsin correspondence school to try to finish my college degree. I took art classes and craft classes. I had a big psychological breakdown at that time because of the relationship and what I was allowing it to shut off in me. We fought all the time. I went on this horrible progression, from thinking I was going to die to thinking there was going to be a nuclear war, and then settled on a fear of going on airplanes that lasted for six years. There was a huge part of me that wasn't being used. The breakup left me and Snuffy, my Yorkshire terrier, alone in Toronto, but I loved Canada and decided to stay.

Months later, a girlfriend and I went to a small avant-garde theater to see a musical. Suddenly I knew where I belonged—not to mention the fact that I fell in love with the guy who was taking the tickets. Within no time I got a job at the box office of that theater and began to work in their children's play productions. I made sixty dollars a week doing pantomime stories for elementary-school children in Toronto. There were four of us in the company and we drove from school to school in my car. I was back in "show business," in love, and very happy. In the evenings I got hooked on going to play bingo. The early-bird games began at 6:30 P.M. and I would stay till 11:00 at night, five nights a week. I would play sixteen cards at once (the more cards, the better your chances were). I had plastic chips that I carried in a pink and blue bag I crocheted myself. The whole room was filled with smoke. Everybody smoked one cigarette after another and ate potato chips. They would sell hot dogs too, and once I was so into the game that instead of reaching into my bag of chips, I put my hand in the mustard. Like everything else in my life, I got compulsive about the bingo. The most money I ever won was 250 dollars. I probably spent much more than that.

In 1972, a production of the play *Godspell* was going to cast a company in Toronto and there were open auditions. The notice said you had to act out a parable and sing a song you loved to sing. I worked hard on my audition and mastered my favorite song, "Zip-a-Dee-Doo-Dah." I was one of the first people chosen for the Toronto company. It was my first professional job in the theater. I was admitted to the Actors' Equity union for stage performers and I joined an amazing company of talented people who continue to weave their careers into the 1980s, including Paul Shaffer, Martin Short, Victor Garber, Eugene Levy and Andrea Martin.

Godspell was a way of telling the Gospel according to Saint Matthew through song and dance and humor. All of us were clowns learning and acting out the teachings of Jesus. I was always fascinated with Jesus, having studied him through art history, through the Christmas and Easter music I sang at Liggett, and through living in a Catholic neighborhood in Detroit and going to an Episcopalian church with Dibby. I was intrigued by the idea that he did all the suffering, that he took the rap for everyone. I was brought up Jewish, went to Sunday school, learned Hebrew, but along with it I was interested in Jesus and his influence on the world.

For a whole year, eight times a week, Jesus died in *Godspell* and we all suffered with him. I suppose that's why I sometimes wondered about getting cancer. Why do I have to be Jesus? Why all this suffering in my life? Why chemo and losing my hair? Why am I marked for some kind of suffering that I see others aren't going through? To make the connection to Jesus was not so far-fetched because he certainly, as I hear tell, didn't deserve to die in such a gruesome way. So I identified strongly going through the treatments. Once I even joked to people that I would give them a picture of me to hang over their bed, that I suffered for their sins and for whatever they did. Jesus, too, screamed a lot and said, "Why me? Don't let me go through this. Can I get out of this please, Father?" He broke down a bunch of times.

Somehow I felt that I was being put through cancer so I could be an expert on it and I could teach about it. I decided I was meant to help other people who had cancer. As a public figure I could go back out into the world like Jesus and say, "I am still here. I went through this, and I am still here."

My career continued in Canada, and I established myself as a comedienne. I was cast in the Toronto company of Second City, an improvisational comedy troupe based in Chicago, along with Dan Aykroyd, Eugene Levy and Valri Bromfield. All the material for our show came from improvisation. We wrote our sketches on our feet in front of the audience, and rewrote them by repeating performances. We had no costumes or sets, just a few chairs, and hats and glasses to suggest characters. We got our premises from audience suggestions and the emphasis was always on being funny. I was a wreck. I used to have to drink a beer and eat a bag of potato chips not to be nervous. We were just frantic behind stage. Someone was always yelling, "Will you work with me? Let's do this." Somebody would have an idea and say, "Gilda, be in this with me," or "Gilda, don't be in this with me." It was the most stressful thing you could ever imagine. But there's no other training ground like it for comedy writers and performers. Some of the greatest names in comedy today began their careers in Second City. My imagination was taxed to the fullest.

During the many months of chemo, I drew on my improvisational training in my visualizations. I would stand inside my body and take suggestions from my brain. I'd imagine the chemicals as these Russian dancers —Cossack dancers—with big black boots and they'd fold their arms and stomp through my body and kick out any cancer cells that they saw. Or my whole body would be a beautifully appointed restaurant with pink tablecloths and flowers at every table. And then suddenly these big trucks of Cytoxan and cisplatin would come and knock over the tables and make a total mess. But if there were any cancer cells eating at the restaurant, hanging around there, they would be totally wiped out. Then it would take about ten days to set the restaurant back up again. Sometimes my white blood cells, or leukocytes, the ones that are the immune system, would be beautiful California kids, blond and suntanned, healthy and strong. They'd walk along the beach inside my body and if they saw some vagrant, scrungy cancer cell drinking and messing up the beach, they'd smash him on the head and kick him out to sea.

In the early 1970s I was becoming a professional, making a living in show business. It was amazing to me. I never dreamt it would happen. I had a review from a Second City show with a big picture of me on the front page of the entertainment section of the newspaper. The reviewer said that I would be the toast of London and New York in comedy. He projected an amazing future for me. I have seven hundred copies of the article at home if you want one. I was so proud of that article.

Through Second City I met John Belushi and Bill Murray and Harold Ramis. When I went to New York to do *The National Lampoon Show* and we were in rehearsal, I went to a store on the weekend that sold all this weird stuff—crystals and incense and books about astrology and spiritualism. I used to love to shop there because it had weird clothes and in *The Lampoon Show* I needed some weird kind of show-business clothes to wear. The guy who worked there was an expert in astrology and had gone to the University of Michigan, so I struck up a conversation with him. He told me that the people I was involved with and I would become huge stars—energy points or cosmic forces in the universe. It absolutely came true—we became stars.

All during my career in Toronto, a certain young man named Lorne Michaels had his eye on me. In 1969, when I was hooking rugs and trying to be a housewife, I had seen him on television in a comedy show called "The Hart and Lorne Terrific Hour." When NBC gave him the okay for a late-night comedy-variety show in 1975, I was one of the first people he hired. He didn't even know exactly what the show was going to be. There were Muppets, and musical guests, and filmed segments and a celebrity host and a repertory company that came to be called "The Not Ready for Prime Time Players," of which I was one. We were television underdogs, nobodies, bad kids, but we made history. Our names became household words. Lorne used to say we were the Beatles of comedy. Alan Zweibel and I created characters like Emily Litella and Roseanne Roseannadanna, and "Never mind" and

"It's always something" became common expressions through the power of television. Our lives were totally altered. Talk around the set changed from "What kind of dog did you have when you were a kid?" to "What are you naming your corporation?" Suddenly I needed a manager and a lawyer and a secretary and an accountant. Bernie Brillstein became my manager and helped me organize my new life.

The most interesting thing to me as the Not Ready for Prime Time Players became famous was how our modes of transportation changed. In the first year of "Saturday Night Live," we all came to work any way we could—subway, cab, bus. When it was time to go home after a show at 1:30 or 2:00 A.M., we would hail cabs and go to the party and hopefully then get cabs to go home. After the second show, I remember I couldn't get a cab so I walked to the hotel I was staying in till I found an apartment. I went straight from appearing on national television to walking alone on Sixth Avenue at 2:00 A.M.

The second year of "SNL," NBC hired a cab company, and we could call and order cabs—one that would go to the West Side and one that would go downtown—based on where we lived. Jane and Belushi and I all lived downtown so we shared a cab downtown. Laraine and some of the others lived on the West Side and they went there. The third year, we each got our own cab account. Seven cabs were always lined up outside Rockefeller Plaza on a Saturday night. By year four, the producers provided each of us with a limousine. I remember riding downtown on Fifth Avenue with my limousine next to Belushi's limo, and Jane's limo next to that, and all of us would rather have been together, talking. We were waving to each other in the limos. We went from nobody caring how we got home, to each being tucked in a little Tiffany's box to go home. That was how life changed.

After the fourth year, I had enough characters to do a comedy album and a Broadway show. Lorne Michaels produced and directed *Gilda Live* at the Winter Garden Theater in New York. I appeared for seven weeks and then did a week's run in Boston and in Chicago. My name stood out huge and bright on theatrical marquees. I was thrilled. Warner Bros. filmed *Gilda Live* as a movie, and some magazine even referred to me as "America's Sweetheart."

In 1980, I married G. E. Smith, the lead guitarist in the band for *Gilda Live,* and the leader of the "Saturday Night Live" band today. The brilliant musician and the spirited comedienne had a civil ceremony in downtown Manhattan. I wore a crinoline on my head and carried a bouquet of lollipops. G. E. wore his best jeans. We lived in the legendary Dakota apartment building and held each other tight on the night John Lennon was killed.

Throughout my career I felt like the girl in "Rumpelstiltskin," spinning straw into gold. My whole career, whether with the guys or not, I was shut in a room taking any situation and making it funny. Second City was about making anything funny, and in *Godspell* the concept was to take the gospel according to Saint Matthew and teach it through humor. On "Saturday Night Live" we satirized everything—the news, behavior, television. Throughout my career my job was to find what was funny about whatever was going on.

So I began to think that I should do the same thing with cancer. It needed me badly because it has such a terrible reputation. I decided, *Well, if I'm gonna have it, I've gotta find out what could be funny about it. I'm a comedienne.* My life had made me funny and cancer wasn't going to change that. Cancer, I decided, needed a comedienne to come in there and lighten it up.

11.

What's Funny About It

I decided I wanted to videotape my ninth and last chemotherapy. My plan was to have Gene videotape the whole experience—going into my room at the hospital and getting in my bed, getting hooked to IV machines, the whole thing. I thought it would add a little show business to this chemotherapy thing. I also wanted to be photographed while I was asleep getting the treatment because I'd never seen myself. I wanted to see what it looked like—me missing thirty-six hours. I was also having more anxiety before number nine than usual. The eighth treatment had left me with considerable numbness in my hands and feet and now they were going to put more chemicals in and that would mean more side effects. I knew there was no way to get out of it, but I kept hoping, like a criminal, that I would get some reprieve—the governor would call at the last minute or something would intervene. But the Alchemist took my blood and all signs were go.

I'd been counting down my chemos after number five. Four to go, three to go, two to go. Now one. I felt wonderful in between—almost cocky with my good health and weight gain. I loved telling my stories at The Wellness Community every Friday: "The Adventures of the Independent, Baldheaded Chemo Patient." I told them about the day I had just been to my internist for my weekly checkup and blood work. Trips to doctors' offices took up half my life. I had driven myself because I was feeling so good. I pulled up to an intersection and I stopped at the red light. I was wondering why I was having these certain side effects and what would happen with my next treatment. Way in the distance I heard this voice saying, "Why are you waiting?" I went on thinking about my future and handling whatever life dealt out, and I could still hear the voice in the background saying, "Why are you waiting?"

It kept repeating, "Why are you waiting? Why are you waiting?"

Five minutes later, when the honking started, I realized the light was a blinking red light and I was supposed to stop and then go through. There was a long line of drivers all pissed off behind me and they all began to pass me ferociously, giving me the finger through their sun roofs.

I screamed in my car, "Why am I waiting? I'll tell you why I'm waiting. Because I am going through cancer and I am having chemotherapy and because I have so much on my mind and because I shouldn't be driving probably,

I have no right to be on the street but I want to be independent and not a victim."

Later that day at The Wellness Community meeting, a lady was talking about her struggle with cancer, and she said, "Look, nobody knows when somebody is going to die. You could get hit by a car."

I yelled back, "Yeah, and it'll probably be me driving."

Glorious laughter.

Actually, between chemos seven and eight, I totaled Gene's car at an intersection in Santa Monica. I stopped. I looked both ways. I entered the intersection at three miles an hour and almost in slow motion I was colliding with the cutest blue-eyed guy in a Triumph convertible. I turned into Imogene Coca and Lucille Ball. I kept repeating, "My husband's gonna kill me."

The guy recognized me and said he knew who my husband was and he thought he probably wouldn't kill me. Gene's car looked like an accordion. As I pulled away from the accident scene, the hood flew up over the windshield, totally blocking my vision. A gas station attendant helped me tie the hood down and I crept home in what looked like a circus vehicle. Gene didn't kill me. He was just happy I was all right (but he did get very quiet for the two months he drove the rental car while his car was being repaired). When I called the young guy with the Triumph to exchange insurance information, he'd changed his answering machine message to his impersonation of Roseanne Roseannadanna ranting about car accidents, and ending with, "It's always something."

He made me laugh.

Finally, my last chemotherapy day arrived. It would be safe for people to drive in Los Angeles again and the new "take-charge Gilda" was going to capture this one on tape.

On the big day, May 9, 1987, I met a friend for lunch because I knew there would be ten days of me not having my proper taste buds and not enjoying food. So my girlfriend and her husband and I had a nice lunch, and they worked on keeping my mind off what was coming up. I also had to drink a quart and a half of Gatorade that day from noon on so that I could flush out my kidneys. I will never drink Gatorade again, and I intend to dump Gatorade on Jodi's head when this is all over and we've won.

At about three-thirty I went home and packed all my stuff to go to the hospital. Gene came home and set to work making sure the video camera was all prepared and the batteries were charged. We grabbed my overnight stuff and the umbrella with the shoes hanging on it and Sparkle and left for the hospital. I didn't cry. I usually did because I would rather have been going to the airport to get on a plane to go to France or going anyplace other than the hospital, but I had to go through with it. I always went back to the same room at the hospital. There was a familiarity to the whole procedure.

Immediately I had to give up my walking freedom and put on that dumb hospital gown and get hooked up to the IV machine which would continue to flush out my kidneys and hydrate me. Suddenly I thought I was like Howard Hughes in his final days. Without my turban, almost bald, I imagined that I looked like a little old man. I brought three pairs of funny slippers—ones that looked like puffy running shoes, my ballet shoes with watermelons on them, and the pair I bought in England that only grannies wear and cost a dollar. This was all to make the night nurse laugh. Can you imagine me trying to entertain the person in the room when I am asleep? Gene opened up the video camera, got it all set up and realized he'd forgotten to bring a tape. I couldn't believe it. Here we had all the equipment and the battery charged and everything—the cast and the crew and the set and the props—and *no film*. It turned out that there was a security guard working in the hospital who had a tape that he had a couple of movies on, but he had seen the movies and he sold us the tape.

Gene videotaped the room, videotaped Jodi setting things up, videotaped me sitting on the bed. When someone came in to take my blood, Gene videotaped him. We all loved it. It was like a show. We were part of the documentary of the final chemotherapy.

My gynecological oncologist came in and Gene got lots of footage of me just talking to him and asking him the same questions that I asked him every time I saw him. The answers calmed me down and gave me peace of mind. He did talk more about future treatments than he had ever done before, and what would happen when I had my second-look surgery, where they would go inside and do biopsies to see if there was any cancer left. He talked about putting a catheter in my stomach so they could do water washes for the next six months or a year to see if I sloughed off any cancer cells—just another mechanism to check to see if there is a recurrence. I hated the idea of it, but I also saw the value in having one more diagnostic tool.

If we got boring, Gene would go to the dog. Sparkle would be walking around or eating from her bowl. My regular gynecologist came to visit me and we videotaped him. Then it was time for Gene to go home. The evening went really fast because there was so much visiting and so much talking. Gene went home around ten-thirty or quarter to eleven. That was a wrap for the night. Jodi would take over filming the next day.

I lay in my bed. The fun part was over. I tried to be calm. My last chemotherapy. It had once seemed so far away, and now it was here. Bonnie was my night nurse, the same nurse who had been with me the first night I stayed in the hospital over seven months before. She brought me crystals, which she knows a lot about. She left the bag of stones with me so I could go through each one and feel it and look at it in the light.

Bonnie is a registered nurse. She does all the traditional medical duties that her job calls for, but she also believes in the spirit and its healing power. She says she has learned a lot from seeing how well I got after I had been so sick. She has begun to believe in the healing power of scientifically researched medical treatment in combination with spiritual enlightenment and belief.

I, too, have come to believe in both. I know how important those chemicals are to my survival, and yet holding those healing stones got me through that moment. I had started to wear crystals around my neck as reminders of the body's and the spirit's desire and capacity to be well.

Bonnie gave me a sleeping pill at about midnight and then she put in the catheter so I wouldn't have to get up to pee. But I went into tension and never slept the whole night. I just lay there trying to fall asleep and trying visualization, trying to find something to calm me. I thought of everyone at The Wellness Community. I thought about

Joanna, Sparkle, Gene, anything to latch onto for peace of mind. I was just too anxious. Bonnie came in and gave me another half of a pill to put me to sleep.

Before I knew it, it was 6:00 A.M. There were Jodi and Bonnie, hanging bags of chemicals on the IV pole. The first thing they had to do was shoot the steroids into my system. I was suddenly so wide awake that they made me take my three and a half sleeping pills and the Benadryl to go to sleep.

I said, "Don't start the steroids, I'm not asleep"—still trying to control the situation from my helpless position. As soon as the steroids went into the IV, I could feel my whole body go hot. It was such an awful, weird feeling that I pleaded, "Wait till I am asleep. Wait till I am asleep."

I felt the heat go through my body, and that is the last thing I remember. The sleeping pills started to work and I fell sound asleep.

This is what I saw later on tape:

Gene coming down the hall with Sparkle in a tote bag, hiding the dog from other people in the hospital. Then coming in the room. It's about 6:00 P.M. I see me lying there—I look a little like Bruce Willis. My hair is starting to grow in every which way and I am asleep and you just see my head with all the covers all around me. Gene puts Sparkle down on the bed and Sparkle runs and kisses my face and I wake up. Then I see Gene and he kisses me and I kiss Sparkle and they set up my tray table and they bring me something to eat. I murmur something and try to take a bite of the food and fall promptly back to sleep. There is a jump cut.

The Alchemist comes in. He talks to me—I kind of mumble and don't wake up. So he yells, "Did you see the hearing doctor?" He asks me questions while I am asleep. He says again, "Did you have your hearing checked this week, Gilda?" He has a whole loud conversation with me about my hearing. I whine and whimper, "Go away, leave me alone, let me sleep."

The picture fades to black.

Jodi spent twelve hours with me sound asleep. I guess she got bored because she went and got paper from the nurses' station on the floor and started writing things in Magic Marker and putting them near my head and videotaping them. They were like the balloons in cartoons. She got compulsive about it so you see me lying there, sound asleep—so pathetic—and there are note cards saying, "I wonder when Gene and Sparkle are going to come." Or, "Oh, I am so happy this is my last chemotherapy." Some of the thoughts are quite long, like, "I'm really handling this well. Here I have gone through all this and I am doing a great job." It's the same positive attitude that Jodi had been injecting in me since she had gotten the assignment to take care of me. Meanwhile I was just lying there, not even changing positions.

Jump cut—the umbrella with shoes hanging from it is over my head. Jump cut—there are roses all around my head like a wreath on a horse. Jump cut—this horrible Chinese china dog that was always on the coffee table in the room is now sitting on my pillow. It looks just as stupid on my pillow as it did on the coffee table. Jump cut—the gynecological surgeon comes in. He is an angel and we always joke about him because he wears clogs. He is sitting in the chair and you can't believe how panicked he is to be on camera. You begin to wonder how you can let someone operate on you if he can be this nervous. Jodi pans down his body and takes a picture of his feet so you can see his clogs. Jump cut—it's Jodi holding the video camera, looking into the bathroom mirror and holding a sign that says: "This is Gilda's nurse videotaping this."

Two days later, Jodi and I watched the tape. I found it hysterical. Of course it is terribly out of focus and too dark and slow and boring for anyone to watch who isn't the sleeping, balding star. But Jodi and Gene did a magnificent job and everyone at The Wellness Community loved hearing about it.

In May of 1987, my chemos were complete. Six months of cisplatin and Cytoxan had left me very tired. The last chemo wore me out more than any of the other ones. I felt the toll of the constant assault on my body. I felt more side effects than ever and felt clammy for a long time. For the first time I felt like my skin was hanging on my bones. My chest felt heavy and my breathing was short. My feet were totally numb now so that sometimes I felt like I was going to tip over because I wasn't standing on anything. My hands were so numb that I had difficulty writing. The doctors said the numbness would gradually disappear. I threw myself a party to celebrate the end of chemotherapy and midway through the party I was so exhausted I wished everyone would go home. I had a month to go before my second-look surgery.

It seemed that now more than ever my brain filled with anxieties. When chemotherapy is ongoing, you feel like you're doing something about the cancer. When it's finished, you wonder if the cancer is getting away with anything.

At The Wellness Community the next Friday afternoon,

somebody stood up and said that in the Twenty-third Psalm, "The Lord Is My Shepherd," even though it says, "Yea, though I walk through the valley of death," that's no reason to buy a condominium there. I thought that was the funniest joke I'd ever heard. I decided to take action against my own brain. I made up this chant that I could think over and over again so that I wouldn't think of something else. It was just so I'd have these words to think so that the cancer thoughts couldn't get in. I suppose it's like Buddhist chanting, just to close out the mind to other thoughts, but the Gilda version of it.

I started to say to myself, "I am well," because I wanted to be well. And then—for an insecure comedienne this was very difficult to say, but I put it in—"I am wonderful." I was embarrassed about it even though no one else was hearing it. Every time I said the word *wonderful,* I would smile. I knew that smiling a lot helps fight disease. And finally I would say, "I am cancer-free," because that was my goal—the ultimate situation to achieve. So if I woke up in the night and I was scared, or if my thoughts were negative during the day, I would just say, "I am well, I am wonderful, I am cancer-free." It would help me fall back asleep at night if I woke up. I repeated it over and over while I swam in the pool. I spoke it out loud in my car. Those words just happened to work for me. It sounded like a slogan from an advertising company, but it gave me peace of mind.

My friend from The Wellness Community who is my age and also has ovarian cancer was having her second-look surgery just a few days before mine. She was filled with anxiety. We had an emergency lunch to discuss fear

and on the way there in the car I extended my chant into
a song.

> *I am well.*
> *I am wonderful.*
> *I am cancer-free.*
> *No little cancer cell is hiding inside of me.*
> *But if some little cancer cell is sneakily holding on,*
> *I'll bash and beat its fucking head and smash it till*
>   *it's gone.*

12.

The Second Look

Wouldn't you know that I would have the kind of cancer where they have to open you up again? With most cancers, you go through your course of chemo and then you just have to believe that it worked and killed all the cancer cells. I had to have an opening, a second opening, a big show, where they could look in and see, putting a whole lot of opening-night pressure on a very tired Gilda. My friend Helen at The Wellness Community said to me that she was sure that when they opened me up for my second surgery they would find a beautiful restaurant with no cancer cells eating there, that my visualizations would have turned the whole peritoneal cavity into Lutèce.

As the month following the last chemo went by, my strength returned. I could taste wellness. I felt so well that I got depressed because I had to go into the hospital again. I also found that I was angry about the whole second-look surgery. There I was in what I hoped would be the last steps of this cancer, but I hated that I had to take a couple of steps backward in order to go forward again. After the surgery, I would have to wait four days to find out the results of the biopsies. I couldn't help but think about how I would feel if they did find more cancer. I worried that it would destroy my faith in my own sensibility and my sense about my body. I felt so clean and clear and healthy that if they found something, I would really feel out of control. The issue of control plagued me—that despite the war I was waging, and my endurance, I couldn't control the outcome.

Joanna said to me that in a way it didn't matter what happened because I had learned to live with cancer. I had learned that life goes on and you can still feel well and accomplish things, and that I really had nothing to be scared of because I knew, even with cancer, life would go on anyway. It was true. In the last six months my life hadn't stopped. I certainly had days when I didn't feel well, but I also had as many days of joy when I accomplished things—met with old friends, made new friends, rediscovered sex and life with my husband, began writing my book, started managing my home and career again. It wasn't easy. It required a lot of inner strength, and a lot of support. I had to use my imagination to get through it. The most important thing was what I learned from Joanna, not to let my life stop while I was battling cancer. Lots happened that was fun and wonderful while I was in treatment. I laughed and saw movies and read. My life didn't stop. If I had to go through chemotherapy again, I would, because it's an investment in my future. I invested ten days of yuck to get ten good days and then to get forty, fifty or sixty years of life. That was what I wanted.

If there were more cancer, I could handle it, but boy, would I be pissed off. You would hear me screaming wherever you lived. People would hear me stomping and raging everywhere. Enough was enough. I wanted to get on with my good health. I wanted the direction of my life back under my control.

I remember when I was eight years old in Florida, there was the cutest little boy. His name was Mark and he used to ride his bike around our block. He must have been a couple of years older than I was, and he was always riding around the block. This one day I was sitting out on the front porch and he rode by and stopped his bike. He was standing there straddling it with one foot on the curb. He yelled to me, "The other morning I saw you outside in your underwear."

"You did not."

"I did—you were out there right on the front porch in your underwear."

"You did not! I never was!"

He said, "I did."

It went on and on like that, and then he rode away, and I sat there thinking, *Did I go outside in my underwear? Could I have made some horrible mistake? Did I go into a trance or some temporary insanity where I walked out on the front porch in my underwear and Mark happened to be riding on his bike at the same time and saw me?* I made a pact with myself right then, at eight years old, that no one was going to catch me off guard like that again. Mark made me feel out of control and I wanted to be in control. My father's death made me feel out of control, and now cancer had me in its uncertain clutches.

Comedy is very controlling—you are making people laugh. It is there in the phrase "*making* people laugh." You feel completely in control when you hear a wave of laughter coming back at you that you have caused. Probably that's why people in comedy can be so neurotic and have so many problems. Sometimes we talk about it as a need to be loved, but I think with me it was also a need to control. I'll make the decision whether to come out in my underwear or not, and I'll make the decision whether you see it or not. It's like standing in front of a whole group of people and having them under your spell, having them in your power, and not letting them get at you first. The hard part about illness and cancer is that it feels so out of control. At The Wellness Community they teach you how to take charge—to participate in your fight for recovery. But they are careful to explain that participation can become a variable in favor of getting well, but sometimes the outcome of the disease is totally out of a person's control. Whatever happens, it isn't the patient's fault. There are so many overwhelming factors involved —environment, genetics, the progress of medical science. Our own actions can aid in our recovery, but having cancer made me realize that we can't control the outcome.

If the second-look surgery is all clear, I will feel like the most powerful person in the world because I'll feel like I have beaten cancer. It must give you a big sense of confidence because even now I can feel cocky in a way I never have in my life—even pudgy and with no hair. I have my red badge of courage. I feel like I have been so courageous, like I have medals on, like the guys coming back after the war, the confidence they must have felt.

Memorial Day 1987 was the first time I went out anywhere without my head wrapped in a turban. I just felt bold that day. I put on lots of makeup and went to a party in Malibu. There were a few people I didn't know but mostly it was my friends who had been through the whole thing with me. I walked in and they all knew how proud I was of myself. I had a big smile on my face. For some reason my hair was growing straight out with no curls in it. It looked like a long crew cut sticking straight out. A friend at the party said I looked like one of those newborn Easter chicks. Everyone kept patting me on the head. They couldn't resist it because if felt like a baby's downy hair.

I got in a very funny mood, even feisty. They had a big buffet and I took cuts in the line and kept saying "Get out of my way" to everyone. I did it on purpose to make them laugh. I was pushing people in the line and cutting ahead of them, and saying, "Get that spoon out of there!" It was almost like a little child stood up and walked around and started pushing people around. They were laughing.

I walked on the beach. I had had something on my head for over six months. By the ocean I felt that my head was back out in the wind and sunshine. I was happy and felt so clean and fresh. Gene was proud of me, and there was a man there who took a photograph of me. Weeks later he sent me the photo and it was so ugly and dopey I couldn't believe it. You can see right through to my scalp. There are bald places and my face is pudgy and round from steroids. My reflection was ugly, at least in my opinion, but I remember I felt beautiful.

On Wednesday, June 3, the day before my second-look surgery, I felt a little giddy and excited just because I was actually at the last step of the prescribed program. The phones had been ringing all day. It felt just like before opening night in show business. Everybody calling and wishing me luck—break a leg. Feeling the love from people, feeling how strongly they wánted me to succeed. With that kind of support and love, I didn't see how anything bad could possibly happen. My forty-first birthday would be June 28 and I was already planning a huge celebration party with all my friends, my nurses, my doctors and their wives. Gene and I planned to travel back to Connecticut a few weeks after my birthday. We hadn't been there for almost a year.

But I was also terribly nervous. I kept singing my little cancer battle song over and over in my head. I was on an all-liquid diet and down to eating just Popsicles, Jell-O, bouillon cubes, gum and hard candies. Fortunately, these are all my favorite foods. I made a trip to a store called the Bodhi Tree to buy an amethyst crystal. I found a real pretty amethyst crystal that fit right on the chain on my neck, and then I drove back home.

Check-in time at the hospital was 5:00 P.M.—same room, same bed. I had everything packed and ready, and Gene came home and packed to spend the night at the hospital with me. As soon as we got in, I had the usual tests: weighing in, blood tests, and so forth. All were normal. Then came the parade of doctors telling me what would happen the next morning. First came the anesthesiologist, whom I told I wanted to regain consciousness quickly after surgery because the Lakers were playing— the second game of the Boston-Lakers play-off series was at 6:00 P.M., and I wanted to see it no matter what. So he decided to give me some kind of epidural needle so I would be up by 6:00 P.M. to see the game. Aha, the little devil woman still trying to keep control and have her surgery. That evening, Gene slept over in the next room, and we watched TV and laughed, and I actually went to sleep quite peacefully.

At 5:00 A.M., Jodi and my night nurse woke me. More enemas (I'd had them the night before, too). Gene was sleeping peacefully in the next room. By 6:00 A.M. they had me all ready and rolled me down to surgery. There I was on the table in the hallway seeing all my doctors, all the familiar faces in their blue scrub outfits with little blue hats. I had one on, too. I sang my cancer song to the gynecological surgeon. Just as I finished and saw his face brighten up with laughter, I slipped out of the conscious world. The next thing I remember is waking up in the recovery room with Jodi there saying:

"It was all clean."

And then I saw Gene and he said, "It was all clean."

It was all pink and bright and healthy inside just like the terry-cloth towel I had been imagining for the last six months. They still had to check all the biopsies. They had taken biopsies, but the gynecological oncologist said, "Nothing looked suspicious and there weren't any hard parts that were scary. It was all pink and well."

The assistant operating nurse, Joan, was thrilled. She said it was all pink. The whole peritoneal cavity was pink and bright and clear and healthy-looking. Before you knew it, I was back up in my room, and by 6:00 P.M., sure enough, I was watching the Lakers game. Not the best game in the world; the Lakers routed the Celtics again.

During the surgery the doctors had installed a catheter in my stomach in case I needed further treatment and for diagnostic purposes. Previously, I'd received all chemotherapy intravenously. If I needed further treatment, it would be in the form of peritoneal washes where the chemicals would go directly into the peritoneal cavity through this catheter. As a diagnostic procedure, every month water would be passed through the catheter into the cavity and then taken out and checked for cancer cells. These washes are an important advance in monitoring ovarian cancer. And the catheter was comfortable and hardly noticeable.

So we had a little celebration. Gene was on the phone, talking to my mother and my brother with tears in his eyes; nurses were coming to me with tears in their eyes. I lay there contented. In the back of my mind was the fear that something would show up in the biopsies, but the fear couldn't compare with the joy of pinkness.

But major surgery is major surgery. It whips the life out of you. Over the next three days I had so much painkiller that I couldn't tell whether I was feeling good or feeling drugged. The waiting for the lab reports on the biopsies was difficult. Of course I could choose to look at the rest of my life that way, as a time of waiting, waiting for cancer cells to show up. Or I could just live my life each day.

On Monday morning, four days after surgery, I felt the pain of the incision going away. I got all cleaned up, tidied up my hair, put on a little cologne and waited for the doctors. Everybody—the internist, the Alchemist, the gynecological oncologist, the gynecologist, the gynecological surgeon—would be by. I had on a new nightgown that morning and Jodi made my bed with clean sheets. The room seemed fresh.

Jodi was out of the room for a while, and when she came back, she said she had been downstairs at the lab. She had asked the technician who was doing my biopsies what the results were, and he had said, "They're fine, but I want to wait to talk to the gynecological oncologist." It perplexed her, and she told me so. That was the first feeling I got that something was wrong. I could tell that Jodi felt something was wrong.

The next person I remember seeing was the gynecological oncologist. He sat down in the chair by my bed. He is a cute little man, my age or a year older. He sat down across from me and he said, "We have the biopsy reports and they have found that out of the forty-two biopsies, there were two microscopic cancer cells still seen. They were not highly active, malignant cells like you originally had, but they are still on the malignancy spectrum."

He continued by saying the cells were not in my vital organs, but in the pelvic region. The prescribed mode of treatment would be six chemotherapies of cisplatin that would go directly into the peritoneal cavity through my newly installed catheter. The treatments would be a month apart. The side effects wouldn't be as rough as the ones before and he would not administer the chemicals the way the Alchemist had. He didn't believe in giving heavy doses of steroids after treatment to delay the nausea; he thought it was better for the patient to have the side effects and get them over with sooner. So instead of my being sick for ten days, he thought I would be sick for three or four.

He said, "I feel very positive. In your particular case, where the cells were left and how much was left, I am sure we can get them."

And then, very sweetly, he said, "So Gilda, you will just have to put up with me a little bit longer."

He got up and and walked out, but when I looked over at his chair, I saw he had forgotten his briefcase.

It was like a comedy routine. Even though he seemed secure and confident when he was talking to me, very open and direct, he forgot his briefcase. To me it symbolized the uncertainty I would have to live with. This doctor had thought, like everybody else, that there wouldn't be any cancer left. No one ever knows for certain.

A short while later the gynecological surgeon, the one who wears clogs, came in and sat down. He was wonderful. He said, "I have thought about this and I think it's a good thing."

He paused and continued, "I think it's the best thing that could have happened—better than not finding anything."

He said the danger with my type of cancer is that the cells can hide. Most doctors wouldn't have done as many biopsies as they did, he said. They would have done maybe twenty-five and they might have missed the remaining cells, but the cells still would have been there and then I would have had a recurrence in six months to a year or two years. I would have had a recurrence, but I wouldn't have known about it until it grew into tumor size. He said they would have tried to convince me to have these washes, prophylactically, in order to prevent that kind of thing happening, but I probably wouldn't have done it. He was right; I probably wouldn't have. I would have said, "No, I beat this and it's gone away." He said, "Now we can be assured that you'll have these treatments. It's better to know what's there. If there is something else hiding, we'll get it while it's in this microscopic stage."

The truth was that there was nothing remotely like a tumor in there; they would have seen that. Considering what I had had the previous October, my conditon in June was a miracle.

Gene came in shortly after and it was obvious that the doctors had talked to him because he came in filled with joy and spirit and convinced that this was the best thing that could possibly have happened. He said he would so much rather get it now. "Let's fight it now, honey, not six months down the line or two years or five years from now having to go through this again. Let's get the whole thing now."

But there was a pallor over my room, emanating from me. Nobody could cheer me up. I was told I would have the first treatment before I left the hospital, so it was this horrible déjà vu—everything was happening all over again. I thought I would be going home, getting well and going on trips. We had planned to go to Connecticut and then to France and just to get back into life again. My hair was growing back and everything was going to be normal, and suddenly I was given this sentence, another horrible six-month sentence of chemotherapy.

I was totally shattered. All that I had believed was undone. I became terribly depressed. I just wanted to sleep; I didn't want to talk to anybody. I just couldn't believe it. I was furious that the cancer was so insidious, that it had tricked me; that this journey wasn't over. I had to think about mortality again, that I could actually die from this disease. And cancer was controlling me, again. Here it was June and we were talking about more treatments till November. How could I believe that this series would work when I had believed so much that the other treatments would work? My friend with the ovarian cancer called and told me that her second-look surgery showed no sign of cancer. I was so jealous that I didn't know what to believe anymore. Everyone around me was so positive, saying, "This is the best thing." I didn't believe that. I didn't trust anybody. I didn't want to hear about it. I hated the world.

Thursday night was the next Lakers-Celtics play-off game and I asked if they could please wait till the end of the game before my treatment. The gynecological oncologist came and ate dinner with Gene. It was Gene's birthday. At about nine-thirty when the game was over (I don't even remember who won), Jodi gave me sleeping pills and even an injection, but I just couldn't fall asleep. I was so tense. Then all of a sudden I lost control of my bowels. I had diarrhea all over the bed. I remember saying, "Jodi, clean me up. Clean me up."

I asked Gene to leave. I saw panic come onto his face, but I couldn't help it now. So he left, and took Sparkle, too. Afterward I remember Jodi giving me the steroids, the shot that made my whole body go hot. I remember her face when she gave it to me. She knew she had to give me the chemo. For three days afterward I ran a high fever, and every time I woke up, my mouth filled with warm saliva and I threw up. My eyes would fill with tears. I felt in the middle of some endless horrible experiment.

13.

"Delicious Ambiguity"

When *Gilda Live* opened in Boston, in 1979, the morning paper had a review with a headline that said, "Gilda Radner Has No Talent—Zip, Zilch, Zero." Show business is a gamble. There is no certainty. I was beginning to learn that oncology is the same. When I got home from the hospital a few days after the treatment, I kept running a low-grade fever. I was tremendously depressed. I couldn't get out of bed. I lost my appetite. I was like everybody's idea of what a cancer patient is—someone who is losing interest in life. The depression grew and then an even more horrible thing happened—fear entered. In this whole cancer experience up to this point I had managed to avoid fear—the kind that makes you sick to your stomach and pale. Now, a panic set in that cancer was going to kill me. I was going to die. The two microscopic cells became bigger in my mind and more insidious. They were out to get me. They were smarter than me. I was the guy eating a plate of spaghetti in a restaurant and the Mafia hit men stroll in and suddenly he realizes he is going to be killed. I always hated that scene in the movies. The look on the guy's face when there is no way to get out—that frightened look is the way I felt, even though everybody was telling me differently and the actual facts in my case indicated I wasn't likely to die.

I had gotten depressed before—horribly depressed about my hair, depressed about my image, depressed about not being able to have a child, depressed about my body—but I had never felt this sense of panic. It was as though now was the first time I really started to deal with cancer. I wanted to get back that feeling of total omnipotent belief that I would win over cancer. I wanted the omnipotent belief back because it made my life bearable. I couldn't deal with the premise that after you have done everything right, done everything you could possibly do —positive thinking, crystals, visualization, psychotherapy, gotten your head into a wonderful place, everything— suddenly it turns out that perfect behavior might not have worked. I was infuriated.

In discussing it with Joanna Bull, I was like a child, stamping my feet and hating the fact that I didn't have control of the whole situation. Joanna said one of her main purposes in working with me was always to remind me to leave open the possibility of ambiguity in life; that you just cannot know for sure, you can't have everything be perfect, and you can't control everything. You are not responsible for everything that happens nor can you change everything that happens. A child doesn't want to hear that. Joanna has worked so much with cancer patients and people who are living with cancer that she knows there are no certainties. Everyone has to live with the unknowns.

The more I protested about this ambiguity, the more Joanna pointed out to me that it was both a terrible and wonderful part of life: terrible because you can't count on anything for sure—like certain good health and no possibility of cancer; wonderful because no human being knows when another is going to die—no doctor can absolutely predict the outcome of a disease. The only thing that is certain is change. Joanna calls all of this "delicious ambiguity."

"Couldn't there be comfort and freedom in no one knowing the outcome of anything and all things being possible?" she asked. Was I convinced? Not completely. I still wanted to believe in magic thinking. But I was intrigued.

I decided to cancel my forty-first birthday party. I didn't want to celebrate. My best girlfriend, Judy, flew in from Toronto to see me. Judy and I grew up in Detroit and have known each other since we were eight years old, although we didn't become best friends till we were sixteen. Through the years, our lives have intertwined in zillions of memories—school and camp and trips and boys. Now Judy is married and has her own business in Toronto. When Gene would describe me over the phone to her, he would sound so bleak that she wanted to see me in person.

People really don't know much about cancer if they or someone close to them doesn't have it. So here came my girlfriend Judy in a panic.

"Did you come here because you think I'm going to die?"

"No, don't talk stupid," she said.

Judy and Gene and I went to see the gynecological oncologist. He laid things straight on the line for us. He said that he felt that in my case these peritoneal washes would work. He said statistics on these treatments were minimal because they hadn't been used long enough for there to be any long-term data on them, but he was confident they would work, especially in cases of microscopic cancer, like mine. As for the increasing numbness in my hands and feet and the potential hearing loss, he said he would moderate all that carefully and make a choice if the side effects became irreversible. Finally he said, "I'll worry about the cancer, you just worry about getting well."

Judy was relieved, and she liked the way the gynecological oncologist talked. She had never heard of these peritoneal washes before. But at least she didn't think I was getting voodoo done to me, and she finally admitted that she *had* come because she had thought I was going to die. I realized that she didn't know anything about cancer and was as frightened of it as anyone. I realized that I am affected by other people's fear—like when I see somebody who is really afraid of cancer, I'll think that person knows something about me that I don't know, when the truth is, I am the expert, I'm the one going through it. It makes me angry at first, then just sad. All through our lives Judy and I protected each other. If one said to the other that everything was going to be okay, we could believe it. If I was flying somewhere and Judy wasn't, I'd be sure to tell her so she could worry about me, and I'd do the same for her. We believed that somehow this would protect us. It seems childish, I suppose, but now it's a shock to me that it doesn't work. I think all my childhood beliefs and all the child in me have been devastated, just knocked unconscious.

When Judy left she felt better about everything. I didn't. Even though almost a month had passed, I was still having anxiety and making myself nauseous with fear.

One night, about a week after Judy had gone back to Toronto, I was getting into bed with Gene. Sparkle was curled up at my feet and the lights were on. I pulled the covers up around me and began to whimper.

"Help me—please help me, I'm so scared. I don't know what to do—I am just petrified, I'm panicked."

And Gene turned over and said, "I can't help you—I'm tired of helping you. Why don't you worry about something besides yourself? Worry about me—worry about the dog. Just get off yourself; I can't help you anymore. You're mean and cranky and inconsiderate all day and then at night you get in bed and you get frightened and panic and you want me to make everything be all right and I can't."

Tears started to well up in my eyes. I was being rejected. Gene wasn't going to parent me or soothe me. He was confronting me, and in less than a moment my tears changed to anger. I turned to him and attacked.

"You're a self-centered, oversensitive bastard."

I started to get very strong and screamed at him things like, "You don't know what it's like to go through this—

you bellyache if you have a little pain in your back or a scratch or a cut!"

In my venomous yelling, I thought to myself, *Who cares if he leaves me? If I have to go through this whole thing myself, I'll go through it by myself.* But at the same time I was thinking, *Where will I move? Can I get him to leave this house while I stay here?* Then another part of me was crying inside—*Oh no, I can't do it myself.* But I kept saying horrible things to Gene—mean and vengeful. Suddenly it was like our relationship was on the line instead of me being afraid I was going to die from cancer.

"You can leave me—leave me if you want—or are you afraid to leave someone who is dying of cancer?"

I said that out loud, so dramatically that it was still ringing through the air after my mouth was closed; me viciously using my own fear to win an argument. Saying it out loud was like bringing the monster right into the room. Then neither of us said anything. It was quiet in the room and we were just lying there, both tired. Before we went to sleep I reached over and took Gene's hand and he held my hand back.

In the morning when I woke up, I felt better. I didn't feel frightened. A couple of times during the morning I tested to see if I was still frightened. I tried to be frightened again, but it wasn't there. I felt that kind of old omnipotence coming back. I felt cocky and I started to see the cancer cells as really tiny and I thought, *I can get through the treatments and I can wipe them out and they're not going to get me.* I thought, *I am going to work harder. I am going to meditate twice a day. I am going to be more positive.* I said to Grace that I wanted to go into Westwood and go shopping and see people. My desk had piled up and I had phone messages to return. When I had first come back from the hosptial ten days before, I had had forty-five minutes of messages on my phone machine. At first everyone was calling to say "Congratulations." Then the same people were calling back to say "Hang in there" after they had heard that I still had microscopic disease and more chemo was in store.

It took Gene a couple of days to recuperate from our fight. How quickly the universe can embrace opposites. I realized I was strong enough to risk my marriage. I almost wanted to be alone—because then maybe I wouldn't feel so totally dependent. I was tired of that. It was so good that Gene yelled back at me. It made me feel like a person. If Gene thought I could take it, then I wasn't dying. People whimpering and hovering over me made me feel like I was dying. People yelling at me made me feel alive.

I decided I could handle these next chemos, that they wouldn't be so bad. My hair was growing back and my face looked more normal. I was lucky. What I had left of this old rotten cancer was treatable, and I was young and fit and could withstand the battle. I started to visualize a huge question mark with me crawling all over it, kissing it, embracing it, loving the unknown. The cancer war would continue and I was right in the middle of the action—but I was armed. I had tremendous will. I had tremendous strength.

I remember the lessons I had learned at The Wellness Community, everything Joanna had taught me. There will always be blood tests and X-rays and CAT scans and uncertainty. The goal is to live a full, productive life even with all that ambiguity. No matter what happens, whether the cancer never flares up again or whether you die, the important thing is that the days that you have had you will have *lived.* It's a hard concept, and it doesn't mean denying the depression and anger that come with cancer. But I've learned what I can control is whether I am going to live a day in fear and depression and panic, or whether I am going to attack the day and make it as good a day, as wonderful a day, as I can.

I told Gene I wanted to keep our plans to go to the south of France after the third chemo of this new series, and maybe go back to Connecticut between chemos three and four. I thought that my book would have to be longer now—more chapters, more information, much braver stories to tell. Whenever I got a bad review on an opening night the only antidote was to go back out and do the show again, to have courage and not let fear destroy me. So if the "Gilda Radner Show" that was my life had to have cancer in it, cancer wasn't going to steal the limelight.

The south of France was beautiful in September. Everything seemed bigger than life—every sunset, every bit of sunshine, the way the roses smelled and opened in the light, the way the pool felt when I got into it. I loved to see tiny Sparkle riding in my purse while we shopped in the thirteenth-century villages. Gene and I had warm butter croissants and brioches for breakfast with homemade jams and huge mugs of coffee and warm milk. We played tennis every day and I learned to yell "Good shot" at the top my lungs every time I missed the ball while running on numb legs. We ate lunch outside under cherry trees at tables with white cloths and yellow napkins. We drank wine at lunch and spent the afternoons reading and whispering and giggling at Sparkle's attempts to guard the pool.

We made love in the late afternoons and dressed for dinner—Gene in jacket and tie, and me in my new linen dresses and red high heels. I put mousses and gels in my very avant-garde, short hair. Sparkle always got new bows in her hair and sat right at the table with us. She is quite a celebrity in the south of France. We went to the village where we were married three years before. We bought ice cream cones and talked about the future, all the possibilities of that delicious ambiguity.

After my fourth chemo, I went back to Connecticut. I went alone with Sparkle. Gene had work in California. It was October in New England—Indian summer—warm days with spectacularly colored leaves. I stayed two weeks. Judy and her husband and baby came for a week and so did my girlfriend Pam from Boston, and my mother and brother flew in from Detroit. They hadn't seen me for the whole year, and they didn't believe that I had been sick when they saw how well I looked and how active I was. My mother was so joyful, and my brother was relieved. He had been sending me a card or letter every day for a year.

My stay in Connecticut turned into a celebration. We had fires in the fireplace and walked in the leaves and cooked meals and they all let me take care of them. My house again became what it had always been—a resort for my friends and family. I was taking care of people again instead of being taken care of. It was so important to me.

The Connecticut house is really my home, where all the things are that make up my history. I bought it in

1981 with money from the movie *Hanky Panky*, the movie where Gene and I met. It's an old house, over two hundred years old, on beautiful grounds that punctuate every season dramatically. I bloom there. The fact that I made it back there after my long illness in California was a miracle. I would go out to the neighborhood stores just to shock people when I walked in the door. I'd go in with a dopey smile on my face because I knew I would surprise them, and they would leave the cash register and come running out to hug me. The week before I came home, I think there was an article in the *Enquirer* that said I weighed eighty pounds and my arms were like sticks and I was dying. I think the *Enquirer* gets its information from washroom walls. So for me to walk in tan and looking healthy was a shock. In my local supermarket all the checkout people went nuts when they saw me. The manager yelled "God bless you!" and he threw a case of toilet paper in the air.

After my stay in Connecticut, I came back to L.A. for my fifth chemotherapy treatment. I was filled with confidence. I had two treatments left. I knew I could get through it. Christmas was coming. I would be done by Christmas—a piece of cake. It took me just a week to get over these treatments. I would have one treatment in November, then I would do all my shopping, and I would have the next one, and then I would be fine by Christmas. I was skipping and spinning with happiness. I was making plans about working, and thinking about the future really strongly. I could smell wellness again. Two days before my fifth chemo I had my hearing checked to be sure it was all right. Then I went to the neurologist and he did tests on my nerves, sticking pins in me like a voodoo doll. The numbness had increased a lot in my arms and legs. My legs, which had been numb below the knee, were now numb above the knee into the thigh. I had noticed it, but I had gotten used to it. When I walked on my feet it felt like I had on huge boots filled with sand. My arms were numb almost to the shoulder. I could still play tennis, but when I would feel in my pockets, I couldn't distinguish between objects. I had also found it hard to type because I couldn't feel the keys well.

Other people might have had these side effects and thought they were going out of their minds, but I just got used to them because they were so gradual in coming. But when the neurologist finished the tests, he looked at Jodi and me and said, "I can't guarantee that after the next treatment you won't have irreversible damage. Right now the damage you have is livable and some of it is reversible, but your nerves are so toxic from this continual assault that the next treatment could do damage that will make you disabled. Some people don't have any toxicity to the nerves. In your case, it is getting extreme."

He said he was going to confer with the gynecological oncologist about the risk of disabling me while they were trying to kill the cancer. Jodi and I went out to lunch. I cried and we speculated about what would happen. I knew I was facing another crisis.

The night before the scheduled chemo, the gynecological oncologist called me at home and said, "No more. We are done with the chemo. That's it."

A part of me sighed with relief—no more of those weird chemicals, no more hospital stays.

But then he said, "We are going to do six weeks of radiation therapy."

I screamed, "What are you talking about?"

"I can't tell you at this point with certainty that there might not be some microscopic cancer left. We must complete a modality of treatment in cancer therapy. If six chemos are prescribed, then you have to finish the entire six treatments. So I want to move to another modality of treatment. You will have thirty radiation treatments over a six-week period. Then I can feel we have done everything possible to eradicate the possibility of a recurrence. You'll have a belt and suspenders holding up your good health."

I said, "I thought I had these two little microscopic cells left. Isn't radiation a pretty radical treatment for that?"

I panicked. I started to yell in a rage, "I won't do it. Don't you *get* cancer from radiation? Why are you doing this to me?"

And he kept saying, "We are talking about curing you. This is not a desperate effort to capture a raging cancer; this is for a cure. To cure cancer you have to treat it progressively, and because you are young and can take it, I want to give you every treatment possible. I don't want there to be a recurrence in two years. I want to get rid of it now!"

Again I was arguing with a man who was trying to save my life. He had to win. I hung up the phone. I went into my room. Everyone was petrified of me, Gene, Grace, Jodi. I slammed the doors in my room and I screamed and swore and yelled. I broke bottles of cosmetics and I threw books against the walls. I tried to pierce the universe with my anger. It was such a horrible sentence— another sentence, six weeks, going every day to be radiated. I thought about what radiation meant to me: my father's brain tumor. I had worried about nuclear war, and now I was going to be radiated, like the victims of the bomb.

I ran to The Wellness Community two days later and cross-examined everyone who had had radiation. "What was it like? What were the side effects?" Every question in the world. They erased my fears, but I still came into the radiotherapy department with six three-by-five index cards of questions, starting with "What is the effectivity rate of the treatments? What are the possible side effects? How do I treat them and manage them? What times are available and how can I work treatments into my life?" and ending with "Do you validate for parking?" This was my Wellness Community training. I wanted to know what was going on.

I had a chip on my shoulder—and a lump in my throat. I cried through the whole setup. The technicians marked my body front and back with small dots to line me up for a thirty-second radiation treatment—like a long X-ray— on an area from below my breasts to my crotch on the front, and the equivalent on the back. I hated everyone: the technicians, the radiologist, the nurses, even the physicist who made the blocks that protected my vital organs from the radiation treatment. Even in my agony I realized that they had a certain pride about radiation versus chemotherapy. They felt that radiation had a bad name because of the association with bombs and Hiroshima and so forth, but that it's really a very effective treatment for cancer. They are proud of radiation therapy. At least I had the sense to notice that.

I started treatments on a Monday, November 2, and I

was mean. Mind you, it was "Gilda-mean" who was angry but I still wanted people to like me. I loved being angry at the radiologist for some reason. It wasn't his fault, he was just trying to help me out, but I liked being angry at him. I wouldn't believe anybody. I was feisty on the table when they would lay me down. I found out that if I wore loose clothes I could pick up my clothes and have the radiation without having to put on a hospital gown. I brought my crystal with me every day, and I held it and a photo of Gene and Sparkle. The technicians would line me up and I would say things nervously, like "Just get it right, don't blow it. Just get the areas you are supposed to and don't hit anything else. I'm watching where you put the blocks. Please don't make any mistakes."

At home, I hung thirty squares of toilet paper on the bathroom door and tore off a square after each day of treatment.

By Friday of the first week, treatment five, I had all the technicians' marks and Magic Marker lines on my stomach so I put a Post-it note on myself that said "TGIF." When I picked up my clothes for treatment, all the technicians became hysterical laughing. I broke through the ice of my being the horrible person who was going to be mad for six weeks. They were so happy. Then I sang them my songs about killing all the cancer cells and they opened up. Their faces changed. They all became individuals to me. All this warmth came out, and I learned once again that cancer is what you make of it. If you make it a horrible situation, so will everyone around you. I had put humor into it and I opened the technicians up to their humor. Bob, the head radiation technician, is the funniest person I have ever met, and I have met a lot of funny people. I have had my finger on the pulse of it, and he is the funniest person I know. People who know him there say that he should be on television, but I said, "No, he should be in the radiation therapy department because that is where his humor is needed most." Every day when I came in at three o'clock, he sang me an original song he had written about killing cancer cells or life in the radiotherapy department. They were always to the same tune, "Ghost Riders in the Sky." He would make me laugh so hard that I started looking forward to coming in. I made an envelope that I called "Songs by Bob" so he had to do a song every day. I was admitted as Lorna Blake and all my blocks and X-rays were marked "Blake," but Bob always called me "Mrs. Doone," after the cookie.

I was nauseous a lot. I was radiated abdominally; that's what causes the nausea. The radiation triggers something in the brain that makes you get sick. Not only that, it made me feel repulsed by food. Not that I was nauseous all the time, but I got anorexic; that is one of the side effects of abdominal radiation. It doesn't happen to everyone, but it did to me. Even now I have to be careful not to talk about it because I'll get sick remembering it.

I learned how to treat the nausea with medications. I would come home and right away take something and go to sleep, sleep through the bad part, and then get up. I would be okay in the evenings. But as the weeks went on, some of the rays were hitting my bladder and that made the bladder burn. I could feel it all the time like I had to pee. It burned like cystitis or a bladder infection, but it wasn't. By the end of the treatments I was so tired that even when I'd get up and wash my face, I would be out of breath and have to go lie down. Grace had to drive me. I couldn't do anything. I just wanted to sleep and lie around. At the hospital, I would put a scarf around my mouth because the smell of the place or anything could make me sick. Yet I would still latch onto Bob and his humor. I have a theory now that cancer cells hate laughter and jokes and songs and dancing. They want to leave when too much of that is going on. They love gloom and depression and sadness and fear, but joy makes them want to move out.

Six weeks is a long time, a very long time, at least when you're having radiation therapy. Midway through it I was still driving, but Grace always went with me. One day, we got to the parking lot of the hospital and there were no spaces. Somebody behind me was real impatient and real miserable and yelled from his car, "Hey you, move!" like I was a stupid idiot.

I said to Grace, "There was a time at the height of 'Saturday Night Live' when I couldn't even walk down the street in New York because every single person recognized me and wanted to come up and say hello or wanted to stare at me or ask me something. It got so that I didn't even go out because of that kind of attention. I was so popular. Now I've come full circle to 'Hey you, move!' in the parking lot of a hospital."

I wasn't a celebrity; I was just someone in somebody's way. That's how I felt. I wasn't sad; I was kind of glad for the experience of having gone all the way around life that way.

On December 11, when I went in to have the final radiation treatment, I brought cupcakes for everyone because it was near Christmas. Gene had never gone with me to radiation because it came in the middle of the day, but this day he surprised me and showed up. Everyone was thrilled. He was a movie star and everyone wanted to meet him. Bob got all red in the face and everything, and said, "How do you do, Mr. Wilder? We love you in your films."

Gene came in and looked over the machines. He was so sweet; I remember he looked at each person he met and let them all be proud of their jobs. He'd heard me talk so much about everyone that it was like he knew them. Then they all left the room and I had my treatment, and Gene watched from the control room. I think I was actually singing while I was getting treated. I knew I was on a small television monitor in the other room and it would make a better show if I was singing. When my treatment was done, that final one, they all came in—all the technicians and the radiologist, the physicist and the nurses. They had flowers for me to hold in my arm, like Miss America. They all applauded because I had completed my thirty treatments. They took out time to honor me. I got off the table holding my flowers, and I made them sing the Miss America song that Bert Parks used to sing.

As I looked at Bob and the other technicians I felt like Dorothy in *The Wizard of Oz*. These people had taken me through this journey and had been my friends. Bob was the Scarecrow because I remember Dorothy said to him, "I think I'll miss you most of all." They had written me a card of congratulations. It was a milestone in my life accomplishing what was necessary to save it. No one stood there and said, "Now you're cured," "It's all over," "The cancer is gone." There were no parents or doctors or teachers or professors to say, "You are cured," "There is no more cancer," "It's over." I knew that nobody could tell me that. I felt that I had had all the best medical treatment I could possibly have and inside me I visualized that my white cells were beaming, functioning perfectly, dancing through my body in the vivid colors of Munchkin Land, singing at the top of their lungs, "Ding dong, the Witch is dead! Which old witch? The Wicked Witch. Ding dong, the Wicked Witch is dead!"

14.
Life

It was Christmas 1987, and there I was, done with treatment—no more tortures left. I was happier than I'd ever been in my life. The cancer was behind me and my health was returning. My appetite came back and I ate an entire honey-baked ham over a week at Christmastime. I must have been the only person who for Christmas '87 had to gain about fifteen pounds. It was glorious. People said, "What do you want for Christmas?" and all I wanted was milk chocolates—a double-layer box. I enjoyed that holiday so much because there was really something to celebrate. New Year's Eve we all went out to dinner, Grace and Gene and our cousin, Buddy. We toasted 1988; what a year it was going to be after all this hardship. We were in the clear now. We would be free.

Our plan was to stay in L.A. and then go back to Connecticut in March and to stay there through the summer. I began to exercise regularly and to work seriously on my book every day. At The Wellness Community, I tried to be more active as a fund-raiser. In the beginning of January, *Life* magazine asked me to be on the cover for an interview that I had done about The Wellness Community months before. I didn't want it to be an article about me, but when I spoke to Harold Benjamin, he said that with me on the cover the article would get so much more attention and that would be wonderful and would help so many people. I had to look in the mirror. I looked at my face and thought, *How does my face look? Do I want it on the cover of a magazine?* Then I thought, *Yeah, it's time. It's time to do it.* *Life* magazine was very wonderful about it, although they kept calling up and asking questions like, "Why do you eat tuna fish for lunch all the time?"

I said, "But this article is supposed to be about The Wellness Community."

But they still were calling up and asking, "Well, what does Gene think about the tuna-fish thing?"

I knew they had to emphasize the celebrity angle, but I also felt they would do The Wellness Community justice. The journalist who was reporting the story had done a lot of research there, and it was a great opportunity to give the Community national recognition. Suddenly I was going from radiation, which ended on December 11, to a photo session in January in downtown L.A. in a big studio with a professional photographer. I brought all my clothes and a makeup person and a PR woman to help me out—all for a March release of the article. I got myself together to do it. I wanted to look great on the cover. I wanted to wear suspenders because the gynecological oncologist had said that if I had radiation, then that would give me a belt and suspenders assurance against the cancer ever coming back. So I wanted everyone to see that my health, like my pants, would hold up.

That was my first photo session in three years (I don't count X-rays), and out of all the pictures there wasn't one the publisher wanted because I looked so strained. There was stress in my face. You could see that I was nervous and I pushed too hard. They sent me the only photo they could consider using, and it looked like "coping with cancer" to me. I didn't want a "coping with cancer" cover because that's not the way I was dealing with cancer. I wasn't coping, I was fighting. We agreed to do another photo session to get what *Life* and I both wanted. Less than a week later, I had another session where the photographer came to my house and he was wonderful. He made me feel at ease and less like a celebrity posing for a cover photo. It was more comforting. He took a series of photos that were really wonderful and there were lots of choices. The photo that ultimately became the cover made me proud because I had a confident attitude—and my suspenders.

The magazine came out the third week in February 1988. I loved seeing it on magazine racks, but I especially loved seeing it on the table in doctors' waiting rooms. I was very happy with the article although I had a hard time reading beyond the third paragraph where it said that there's only a thirty-percent chance of surviving ovarian cancer and that I wouldn't know for at least a year and a half whether I was really in remission. The journalist never discussed those statistics with me. That's all I could see in the whole wonderful article about The Wellness Community and about me. I remember I said to Gene, "What do they mean? What do *they* know—they don't know!" I said it to my doctor and he said, "But you *are* the thirty percent, Gilda." That's all my other friends with ovarian cancer could see in the article, too—that one little statistic, which, I understand, makes it a better story. There were great pictures of The Wellness Community. It was wonderful to know that so soon I could go back out and help people, that I was already on the cover of *Life* magazine. The Wellness Community was excited about it and the *Life* photographers began going there all the time. They felt like celebrities, and I thanked Harold Benjamin for making me into a star again, too.

February was a grand month in other ways, too. Gene and I took a vacation at a health spa near San Diego. We played tennis and swam and even danced in the nightclub after dinner. I made plans with my friend Alan Zweibel to do a guest appearance on "It's Garry Shandling's Show." Alan is the producer and Garry is a friend as well. As a matter of fact, sixteen months earlier I'd been on my way to do the show when I got put in the hospital with the original cancer. The show had become a big success and it seemed fitting that I return to television with Zweibel by my side, the writer with whom I created many of my "Saturday Night Live" characters. We would rehearse the show March 2 through March 7 and shoot it on March 8. It had been eight years since I'd been on television and it passed through my mind that I should be scared, but after what I'd been through, that seemed crazy.

On February 22 I was the guest speaker at a fundraising luncheon for the Friends of The Wellness Community. When I got back home about two-thirty in the afternoon I had a stomachache. I felt funny and weird in my intestine. I called up the Alchemist and he said I'd better come in. He took an X-ray of my bowels and they could see that some air was trapped. There was a little bit of an obstruction. The only way you can get rid of that is to rest the bowel by not eating or by using an NG (nasogastric) tube down the nose, which I'd been through once before. I had to go into the hospital that afternoon, which I hated. I went on intravenous liquids so I could rest my bowel until it cleared up. I stayed for two days—I read, I lay there. I was in a good mood but I had gone straight from giving a lecture to checking into the hospital. Not to mention that I was healthily displayed on the cover of *Life* magazine at the same time. I was diagnosed as having "radiation enteritis," an inflammation of the bowel that was a common side effect of the radiotherapy I'd had. At least it wasn't cancer. The only treatment was liquids and soft foods so as not to irritate the lining of the intestine any more.

We taped the Shandling show on March 8, 1988. I wondered what would happen when I made my entrance on the show. My knees were knocking, I didn't know if my legs would work, I didn't know if my body would have the energy, I didn't even know if the audience would know who I was. When Garry opened the door, a calmness came over me like I was suddenly home, back in the TV where I belonged, playing in the brightly lit living room set. I had an amazing amount of energy. I couldn't believe it. I could be Lucy again trying to get into Desi's club act. Zweibel said I hadn't lost a beat. After all I'd been through I had no idea whether I could still be funny. But I *was* funny, I was still really funny, and I was so happy. I thought, *I can still have a career, I could still have a show, it's not too late.* My manager sent the finished tape to the networks and a couple of the cable stations, and right away I got offers to do my own situation comedy without even doing a pilot because they felt that this show was good enough to be the pilot. It showed I still had it. I looked good with my short hair and I could still do physical stuff. When a friend saw the show months later, he said, "I never saw anyone so happy to be alive." I had been on the outside of everything, painfully jealous and wondering if I would ever get back again, and now my career was blooming again.

Three days after we shot the Shandling show, my intestine got more and more uncomfortable and I had to go into the hospital and have that tube with the mercury bag put down my nose again. This time, though, they got the mercury bag out—the right way. But I had to spend eight days in the hospital. They gave me sleeping pills and sedatives because having that tube down my nose made me crazy. They figured, "We'll just drug her up so she doesn't suffer." Gene would come every day but some days I wouldn't even know he was there because I was so drowsy. I couldn't read. I didn't feel like watching television. It was a horrible, horrible time, but it wasn't cancer—I kept saying that to myself. I would come out of it. The doctors said, "This is from the radiation, an inflammation that will clear up."

At home I had to stay on a liquid diet with high-calorie liquid supplements. I accepted my eating handicaps. I didn't make food the center of my world. If we went out to dinner, I had soups and talked a lot while everyone else ate. As a matter of fact, a few weeks later I was the guest speaker at a two-hundred-dollar-a-plate fund-raising dinner for The Wellness Community. We sat down to the dinner and while everyone had the first course, some exotic salad with tropical vegetables in it (none of which I could eat), I had a Lipton Cup-a-Soup packet. They brought me hot water, which was not hot enough for two hundred dollars a plate. When everyone else had the main course, I brought out my can of 330-calorie liquid nutritional supplement from my purse and asked for a glass of crushed ice. I got special enjoyment from the fact that I was sitting next to an oncologist, who could see what food options the cancer treatment had left me.

I made my plane reservation for Connecticut for Saturday, April 9, just for me and Sparkle. Gene would join us later. I would meet my girlfriends Judy and Pam in Connecticut where we could all be nine years old again and laugh and rent movies and pretend we were at camp. Spring would be just beginning and Grace would be there ahead of us to open the house and make it shine.

Five days before I left L.A. to meet my friends, I lost my friend Linda from The Wellness Community—a beautiful woman, forty-six years old and the mother of four children. We had had many Friday lunches together. She'd had everything, chemo, radiation, but the cancer still grew. I was visiting her in the hospital when she died. With all my bravado and all my fight, I could never deal with death—the fact that people do die of cancer. I blocked it out of my mind. I saw cancer as a battle, as a hell, as tortures, whatever, but you didn't die from it. Now here was this beautiful, exquisite young mother who was a real warrior, who fought to the end, who had her knitting beside her bed when she died. She was making an afghan, and I remembered that a month before we'd gone shopping and she had showed me a magazine with a picture of the afghan in it. She still embodied the fighting spirit of The Wellness Community—right before she died, she'd been in Houston investigating bone marrow transplants. The disease raged in her, and it took over, but her will to live made every day of her life grand. She fought against all odds and kept herself beautiful. When she died, she had mascara on and her hair was growing back again after her radiation treatments. I remembered that once she had written me that she hoped we'd grow old together, that we'd have lunch or tea as old women.

I had never seen anybody die. I'd never seen a car accident up close or been in the emergency room of a hospital, but I had called fighting cancer a "war" and now I knew the pain of the casualties. Linda and I were in this war against cancer, and in her case the cancer won. But even though it shortened her life, it never robbed her of her joy.

I had a dream that a very thin and hollow-eyed man in a hospital gown stood on our bed with a hammer ready to bludgeon Gene and Sparkle to death. I ran in and jumped on the bed to stop him. He turned and viciously threw the hammer at me. With great dexterity and finesse, I caught the hammer in my hand. Then I woke up.

Before leaving L.A., I had all my blood work done as well as a saline wash of the peritoneal cavity to check for cancer cells. Everything came back tip-top. I would have to be tested every three to four weeks and the Alchemist gave me the names of two oncologists in Connecticut who could do my follow-up work. Life was zooming. I wasn't tied down to the regimentation of treatments. I loved being back in Connecticut and found myself connecting with other cancer patients and talking about starting a Wellness Community on the East Coast. I continued to work on my book and to think of ideas for my television show. Gene joined me in Connecticut and life was normal—actually the kind of better-than-normal that comes after a hard fight.

Wherever I went, especially in New York, people were always coming up to me. They'd take me aside and say, "I had cancer, I had such-and-such cancer twenty years ago." They all wanted to tell me their stories. The *Life* magazine article had been heavily publicized in New York. There were posters of me at every newsstand and even plastered on the sides of buses—my cover photo, with a caption saying, "A brave Gilda Radner laughs at cancer." I got a little cocky. I always had a twinkle in my eye as though I'd touched the face of God, because that's what I felt like I'd done. I was plenty full of myself. I'd go to bed at night bursting with plans, and I couldn't wait to get up in the morning.

After about three weeks I looked at the names of Connecticut oncologists and called one because he was convenient to get to. I knew I had to get my blood work done. The major blood test for ovarian cancer is called a CA-125. It registers a certain chemical that everyone has but that increases in your blood if you have tumor activity. Any reading of less than 35 is normal. It takes a week to get the test results. They took my blood at the office and the doctor examined me. If I complained of any pain or discomfort, this Connecticut oncologist would mention that it *could* be the cancer. I didn't like him: he was gruff and impatient. I felt like his meter was running while I was talking to him—maybe because I was Gilda Radner I made him nervous. He was about my age. I knew my case backward and forward and told him everything I'd been through and where I was at, and then I told him about the bowel problems. He said that there was a nutritionist he'd like me to see. He said that he could do the diagnostic peritoneal washes right in his office, and he cleaned my Port-A-Caths because they need to be flushed every three weeks.

So I made my cancer pit stop, which is an absolute necessity for all cancer patients. Once you've had this disease, it goes on your whole life. You have to keep getting checked. Then I forgot all about it as April turned into my favorite month, May. I've always liked May because of the lilacs blooming and the beautiful flowers everywhere. I've just always loved it. My neighbor makes ceramic jewelry and she was having a ladies' luncheon to show her work. It was Tuesday, May 3. I was going over around lunchtime. At eleven o'clock I was upstairs taking a bath and washing my hair when the phone rang. Grace yelled up to me, "Gilda, it's for you." It was the Connecticut oncologist. I picked up the phone and he said, "Gilda, I'd like you to come into the office."

"Why?"

"We'll talk when you come to the office."

"I'm not coming to the office, tell me over the phone."

"Well, I prefer you come in."

"Well, I want to tell you something—I didn't enjoy meeting you." I just blurted it out. I said, "I didn't like the way you talked about cancer. You scared me unnecessarily."

He said, "Oh, I apologize for that. Maybe I did speak out of turn."

I said, "It made me very angry and uncomfortable."

"At any rate, Gilda, I would like to see you."

I said impatiently, "Just tell me over the phone."

He said, "Well, your CA-125 has gone up."

"What?"

"Your CA-125 is at 90."

"That's impossible. I just had blood work done in California three weeks ago and it was absolutely normal. There must be something wrong with the test."

It was one of those moments when my heart jumped into my throat. I know the blood must have drained from my face. I couldn't think of anything worse. I continued to fight him.

He said, "I'd like you to meet me at the hospital, and we'll do a CAT scan and some X-rays, and we'll see where it's at."

I said, "I *know* my CA-125 was normal three weeks ago."

He said, "Well, we're not so sure of that."

I screamed, "What are you talking about?"

His voice was emphatic. "Gilda, will you *please* just come down to the hospital?"

"All right."

I hung up the phone and came running down the stairs, and I was screaming for Gene. Bloodcurdling screams. By the time I got to Gene's office, it was like *The Snake Pit* when the woman has gone mad. I was limp with fear and hysterical.

"My CA-125 went up."

"What?"

I saw Gene's face whiten. Grace became paralyzed. Once you have cancer you live on a tightrope, you live from day to day. You talk about how something could happen, something could go wrong. Here on May 3 at eleven o'clock in the morning, my whole world collapsed again. My happy, positive, Wellness Community world fell apart with this doctor that I couldn't stand. I was shaking and crying, and Gene was being very rational, saying, "We don't have enough facts yet. We don't have all the information. You have to get the CAT scan. There could be a mistake." He was looking for every positive thing. Grace was getting ready to drive me to the hospital. Gene is too recognizable so it was best that just Grace and I go. I went upstairs to get dressed, but I was in a trance. It was unbelievable to me that this could be happening.

In the car, Grace was making small talk, but my brain was frozen in the moment when I heard that my CA-125 had gone up. Stuck there, I was just staring. When I got to the hospital, the Connecticut oncologist was waiting there. His presence made me as feisty as a bulldog.

"All right, what do I have to do? What do I have to do?"

He said that he wanted to run a heart test on me.

I said, "What do you mean?"

He said, "If we have to give you Adriamycin, it could do damage to the heart muscle. We want to make sure your heart is in good condition."

"What are you talking about?"

"You're going to have to have treatment."

"Listen, my CA-125 was normal three weeks ago."

Then he said, "It wasn't."

"What do you mean it wasn't?"

"I've spoken to your doctors in California and the computer misread your CA-125 as normal. When it was looked up again yesterday, it showed it was already rising three weeks ago in April."

My CA-125 readings had been around 7 or 8. But in my April checkup in California it had risen to 40 or 45. Now it was 90. The computer had messed up and with all my precious medical care I had become the victim of a computer. My feistiness was melting and Grace just sat there with me, both our mouths hanging open. I went in and I had the heart test. My heart was normal. Then I had a chest X-ray, two sides. Next I drank the barium that you have to drink for the CAT scan. I thought, instead of going to the ceramic jewelry tea party, I'm drinking barium. They gave me the CAT scan. I lay there in the machine trying to do my visualization, my positive thinking. *I'm clean, I'm clear, I'm pink*—I was visualizing the inside of my body as I'd done every day, religiously, for twenty minutes to a half hour once or twice a day. I took my body and from head to toe scraped out any possible cancer cells that were there. I imagined battles going on with armored horsemen killing the cancer cells. My body was clean, I was cancer-free; all the organs were just happy and pink and clean.

As I lay there in the CAT scan machine with the technician saying, "Breathe, don't breathe, breathe, don't breathe," I thought to myself, *I can will this away, I can visualize this away. I will make the pictures be clear, I can control this.* I tried to put all my might and all my power into it. I wanted the results right away. I wasn't going to wait. The Connecticut oncologist said, "Yes, you'll know."

Grace sat in the lobby of the hospital and I paced through the parking lot until I heard the Connecticut oncologist motioning for me to come back in. He took me and Grace into a small waiting room, and he said, "I've gone over your CAT scan and your X-rays with the radiologist. He says you have two nodules of cancer in your upper abdomen on your left side, you have cells on your liver, and you have a shadow on your lung."

I screeched at him, "You mean I'm going to die?"

He said, "No, no"—but in a very uncertain voice. "What you have is treatable. It's not microscopic, but it's treatable."

I said, "What are you talking about?"

And he said, "Well, you have time. You have years. I know a woman, you know, she's three years now being treated."

I saw him close the door on my life in his eyes. I said, "I want you to call my doctors in California."

He said, "I'll be glad to."

He went over to the phone. Meanwhile Grace looked like she had had a lobotomy. I got on the phone with my California gynecological oncologist. He was the person I trusted the most, the "belt and suspenders" doctor, the one who put me on the radiation.

I said, "What am I going to do?"

He said, "What did the doctors there say to do?"

Then the Connecticut oncologist called the Alchemist

and told him the results of the CAT scan. Without even holding the receiver, I could hear his response through the phone. All he said was, "Shit."

Grace brought me home. I don't even remember that ride. It was like I stopped existing. When I got out of the car, I threw up the barium all over the driveway and went into the house and continued to throw up. I just wanted to get into my bed and go to sleep. Gene was asking, "What happened, what happened?" All I could report to him was the most horrific things that could possibly be.

The phone was ringing. Gene had to tell people what had happened. My life had been so active. My manager was calling about the plans for the TV show, and my editor was calling about my book. Half the time when the phone rang it was for me, but now everything stopped. My life faded to black. I didn't talk to anybody. I remember feeling sick from the barium, then nauseous with fear, thinking of my friend Linda dying, and thinking that suddenly I was a terminal cancer patient.

I still held out hope that in California they would help me, that somehow something would turn around. If I just could talk to Jodi, who was out of town. Maybe the new doctor wasn't reading the CAT scan properly. The next day I went back to get the CAT scan to send to California. My gynecological oncologist there had said, "Let me read it." When I went to pick it up the radiologist who had read it was there, and he handed it to me. He had a glum look on his face. He said, "You know, attitude is the most important thing in these cases."

I looked at him and my anger rose to the surface. I said, "Well, that's all I have, buddy!"

15.

Alternatives

"**C**arboplatin," said the Connecticut oncologist.

"Carboplatin is a new derivative of cisplatin. It's supposed to not have the same side effects. It doesn't make you as sick. It's just a different form of the same drug. It hasn't been approved by the FDA yet and it's difficult to get but I can try to get it because I know someone at the drug company who could get it through what is called 'compassionate need.' "

"Compassionate need"—in other words, my life was in danger. When I later spoke to the California gynecological oncologist, he didn't even know how to get carboplatin.

He said, "We can't get it here in California."

I said, "Well, this guy here can get it."

He said, "Oh, well then good, stay there and get it."

When I spoke to the Alchemist, he told me there were a couple of things I should check out myself, including calling a top specialist at the National Cancer Institute in Bethesda, Maryland. I called him.

"Definitely go with carboplatin if you can get it."

I said, "Yes, I can get it here in Connecticut."

He said, "There's a ten- to fifteen-percent chance that it will work to retard the cancer, and I won't say that there aren't a few cases where it has completely arrested the cancer."

He advised using the carboplatin with Cytoxan and warned me that my numbness could increase with this treatment. "Good luck."

The doctors agreed, carboplatin was the way to go. So I put my life in the hands of the Connecticut oncologist who kept giving me assignments like "pee in this jar" and "get this blood test" and "be at this office before ten A.M. on Tuesday" and saying "I got the carboplatin" with an attitude like "look what I did for you!" But I vacillated between feistiness and utter despair, utter hopelessness.

The day before my first carboplatin chemo I went to a local hair salon and had my hair cut as short and close to the head as you can imagine. I thought, *If I'm going to lose it, I don't want to have long hairs all over the place.* My hair was getting long and I had a long tail in the back. I left the tail, but I had the rest chopped off close to my head, almost like a crew cut.

The girl said, "Are you sure you want it this short?"

And I said, "Oh, yeah, I'm doing a *Star Wars* movie."

On May 10 Grace and Gene came with me down to the oncology office where I was to get my carboplatin chemo. It would take about four hours to drip the chemo into my veins. I knew there was cancer growing inside me and I had to do something about it, so I wanted the chemo. But I was haunted by the fact that there was only a ten- to fifteen-percent chance it would work.

Until this point, I had been so sure that cancer was behind me. I'd been through a year of treatment. I had beaten it. I'd been on the cover of *Life* magazine. I had become a symbol of conquering cancer. Right from the beginning, I believed that I would get well. I always saw myself surviving and going back into the world with all my Jesus symbolism, my badge of courage. But it was in these days in May that I suddenly realized I had a life-threatening cancer. Somehow my story of cancer began for real at this point. Through Joanna and The Wellness Community, I had become such an active participant that there was no escaping reality. Now reality was this horrendous nightmare. There was no rationalizing it away.

When my girlfriends would call up, they didn't know what to do. They were just as petrified as I was. Here I'd spent a year telling everyone I would be all right, making everyone else confident and trying to dispel their fears of cancer. Now I was too scared to reassure anyone. When I was first diagnosed, Gene knew what a life-and-death struggle I was in, but I didn't know. Now it was all laid out, no escaping. I was the one who talked to all the doctors. I was awake, I was conscious, and it was all bad news.

My life became crowded with ironies. Weeks before I had been invited into New York by Jane Curtin and Marilyn Suzanne Miller, a writer from the original "Saturday Night Live," for a luncheon in my honor. Neither of them had seen me in seven or eight years and they wanted to celebrate the *Life* magazine article and just have lunch. The carboplatin side effects were minimal—no nausea at all—so ten days later I made the trip to New York for my luncheon. It was all the female staff from "Saturday Night Live" when I'd been there: my costume lady, Margaret, and her sister Elizabeth and my makeup woman, Bobbie, and all the script girls and the secretaries. Everyone was so glad to see me—hugging me and yelling at me because I was too thin and they wanted me to gain weight. They even accepted my dorky haircut. I felt like a fraud. They were all celebrating my recovery, and I was caught in a recurrence. I just couldn't tell them. They took Polaroid pictures and in every one of them I looked like a ghost. Laraine Newman had a cake sent in even though she couldn't be there. All this wonderful food, and I couldn't eat any of it because it was all healthy salads that my radiated intestines couldn't handle.

It was a very bittersweet event, and Jane looked so beautiful. I'd never seen her look more beautiful in all the years that I'd known her. Her personal life was so good—her husband manages her, her child is beautiful —a little replica of her, healthy and bright—and her work is good. I was proud of her—not envious, just proud of her, most of all because she was still Jane. But the luncheon left me feeling like I was a Martian, some outer-space creature who just happened to be there.

When I came home, I had a breakdown. Then Gene and I had a huge fight because I said that I wanted to go to Mexico and have laetrile treatments from apricot pits or something like that. Joanna had sent me a book called *Cancer Survivors* about alternative therapies outside of standard medical treatment. There are about ten treatments described in the book, and of course, after each one I read, I thought, *Well, I'm going to do that!* So there was Gene, hoping we'd have a normal evening, eat dinner and watch a little TV. I turned to him and said, "Will you go to Mexico with me if I have this laetrile?" (I'd just read that chapter in *Cancer Survivors.*)

He flipped out. He had just had it. He said, "No. Absolutely not!"

He said, "I'm not going. No peach pits!" He smashed his dinner plate on the floor. "I'm not going and have you do peach pits!"

I yelled, "Well, what if I'm dying and that was the last resort?"

He yelled back, "I don't care if you're dying, you're not going to have peach pits!" He just got settled on that and because he was saying the wrong fruit—it was apricot pits—that was really driving me crazy. He was going on and on saying the wrong fruit.

"Peach pits, it's crazy!"

I thought, *He's abandoning me.* It was a huge fight. Judy called in the middle of it to see how I was, and I yelled at her. Then I said, "Would you like to go with me to Mexico to have laetrile?" and she said, "Sure."

I turned to Gene and said, "Judy will go with me."

He said, "Well, good, then go with her."

The truth was, I was mad at everyone. When I had called Joanna to tell her about the recurrence, she had been just as sad as me. I hadn't even been able to listen to her talking. I didn't believe in anybody, I didn't believe in anything. It all seemed like bullshit now, everything. I spoke to Harold Benjamin on the phone. He and all my friends at The Wellness Community were all devastated, they were just as devastated as me. I had become a spokeswoman for The Wellness Community, and a symbol of getting well. I had been a model cancer patient completely active in my own therapy. Now I felt like a living example that it didn't work.

I'm just a fraud, I thought. All these people had told me they had taken the *Life* magazine cover and hung it up in their bedrooms to help them get through their treatment, and now I was standing up there with my hands on my hips wearing my suspenders that didn't do any good. I continued to have long talks with Joanna on the phone, but part of me was closed off. Things ran through my mind like the gynecological oncologist saying, "Your tumor must be very aggressive." After all that treatment, it came back. The radiologist had told me that radiation was ninety-percent effective for getting rid of microscopic cancer—ninety-percent effective. Ha!

During the first four weeks after the recurrence, I spent a lot of time lying on the floor and staring at the ceiling. I would come down for breakfast and not be able to eat because I was so frightened. I'd end up just getting off the chair and lying on the floor in the kitchen staring at the ceiling. I didn't know what else to do. It was so hard on the people around me. I'd wake up in the night screaming.

"I'm going to die, I'm going to die! I'm petrified, I'm going to die!"

Gene would say, "You're not, you're not." He kept saying, "This will work, this treatment will work. You've done it before, you'll do it again. I believe in you."

He was continually coaching me, building me up. But when other people called on the phone, I grew to hate their calls. They only reminded me that nothing was happening. I felt they were calling only to find out whether I'd died. I decided they were calling only to make themselves feel better, not me. So I stopped taking phone calls. I didn't want to talk to anyone.

When I went in for the second carboplatin treatment, my CA-125 had gone up from 90 to 135. The cancer was still growing. The Connecticut oncologist said that it would take three treatments to have any effect. But my CA-125 count was so shocking that I couldn't even accept it. Even worse, the carboplatin began to affect my bone marrow. I became very tired and short of breath. I was out of breath when I climbed the stairs in my house. I was so tired that I didn't even have the energy to walk in the yard. I wasn't manufacturing enough blood to carry oxygen throughout my body. The Connecticut oncologist said I'd have to have a blood transfusion. Gene gave blood and so did my neighbor's husband.

What I mourned most was my lost joy, my happiness, my exhilaration with life. I would say to Gene, "I want my joy back, I want my love of life. It's robbed from me. I have to go through treatments, I have to think about this thing growing inside me." I began to have pain around my liver. Then I thought of my life degenerating into pain, then eventually being on a morphine drip, and then dying. The image of my friend Linda dying repeated in my head. I would lie in bed and think I was her.

Then Harold Benjamin did something wonderful. He sent me his World War II bomber wings in an envelope. He had been in the Air Force in the war and these were his real flying wings. He wrote, "I've had these with me since 1944. You keep them for the next forty-four years.

They have done the job for me—they will for you. Love, Harold." They were beautiful and I knew they were something precious to him. In his wisdom, he was telling me, "Just remember you're in a war." When he was flying, he didn't know whether he'd get hit or what would happen to him, but he flew with bravery. I was touched by what he did. I put the wings up near the phone on my desk where I could look at them all the time. They gave me a focus. Harold was reminding me, "You're still in the war. You have to fight more but you can still win."

Then I remembered what The Wellness Community was about. I remembered what Joanna and I had worked on for over a year. There are no guarantees. There are no promises, but there is *you,* and strength inside to fight for recovery. And always there is hope.

So on a day when I felt brave like a soldier, I called a man I'd met in Connecticut who had just been diagnosed with lung cancer. I had called him a few weeks earlier to give him a pep talk. Now, I poured my heart out to him and I said, "I've had a recurrence."

He was so sympathetic, he said, "Gilda, why don't we get together? Why don't we talk? I know a couple of women going through breast cancer who maybe would like to get together, too."

He and his wife had gone on a macrobiotic diet, a carefully balanced diet, more than half of which was composed of whole grains like brown rice. His wife suggested to me that I call this one girl in the area who had cancer but had been on a macrobiotic diet for years, and her cancer had stayed under control. So I called her, too, and I invited everyone to come to my house on a Wednesday night.

I said to Gene, "I'm going to have a Wellness Community meeting."

It was the first time I'd felt happy since the recurrence. I fixed up the living room in a congenial seating arrangement. I had told everybody to come around seven o'clock and that we would meet for two hours. Twelve people showed up. My friend with lung cancer was the only man. I ran the evening just like a Wellness Community sharing group. I explained what The Wellness Community was and what goes on there. Then I said, "Why don't we each go around and tell our story." I said that we should keep what we spoke about in confidence among ourselves and that the purpose was to simply share our experiences with cancer. Like The Wellness Community, it was wonderful—each person told about themselves and where they were at that point and what they'd been through. There were three or four people there who were on macrobiotics and who were very active in the macrobiotic community in New York. They each had different types of cancer. Their experience with macrobiotics was interesting to learn about. I was able to spill my heart to these people, who understood in the deepest way. We decided that we would do this every week. I said, "My house will be open every week on Wednesday from seven to nine o'clock so we can come and talk about what we're going through." I said, "You don't have to call to say whether you're coming. I'll be open."

I felt a great deal of comfort in this group. I didn't feel the need to be funny, but I was. One Wednesday, before the meeting, it was raining. I put on a raincoat and I went out walking on my street. A car went by and splashed this huge amount of mud on me. I was sopping wet, walking down the street. I started talking out loud to myself.

"That's me, 'Cancer Woman'! You can do anything to me. I can walk through storms. I can get splashed by cars. I can have millions of treatments. You can radiate me, you can give me poisons, but you can't destroy me because I'm Cancer Woman!"

The next thing you know, I'm kind of running down the street with my arms spread out in this raincoat yelling in a Captain Midnight voice, "Cancer Woman, look at her go!"

I turned back and more cars went by and splashed me, and I said, "Ha, ha, ha, ha! It's Cancer Woman!"

I came back to my own backyard and went running around. No one else was home. I was running around the backyard being Cancer Woman, making music for myself, "Da, da, da! Da, da, da! She can take it, she can have more cancer and more cancer and the cancer never goes away and the years go by!"

I went on and on. Of course, when I had an audience later I did the whole thing for them, the whole Cancer Woman routine. They laughed because I'm sure they had all felt that way at times.

Grace and Gene were especially relieved to see me happy for the first time in weeks. There was one lady at the meeting who had resigned herself to dying, and I just gave her a huge talking-to, which was the talking-to I needed myself. Of course, three days later I'd lie in bed pretending I was at my own funeral, that I was in a coffin. I would sink back into pits of despair. I was so unpredictable that Grace and Gene had to be like a bomb squad, never knowing what would set me off.

At that first meeting, I was fascinated by the people who talked about the macrobiotic diet. They seemed the least nervous and most in control of their lives. That interested me. I was still having bowel problems and difficulty eating, but I started to talk to them. They were so peaceful and they looked good, and I thought, *Gee, food has always been a problem with me, maybe food is the answer to getting well. Maybe that's the variable that has been destructive in my life.* I remembered that the *Cancer Survivors* book talked about nutrition as an alternative therapy. One of the women said, "You know, I'll be glad to cook some stuff for you to try." She had a book in her purse. "Why don't you read it? It's about macrobiotics and how it's helped a lot of cancer patients and it's cured a lot of people." She was persistent and wonderful.

The next morning she showed up with some foods for me to taste, some macrobiotic cooking. She was a beautiful woman who has lymphoma but has had it under control for quite a few years on a total macrobiotic diet without chemotherapy. She does a lot of cooking, has dinners at her house and is active at the Macrobiotic Center of New York. She just started dropping food off every day, things like rice cream, which is strained brown rice with the husks off. She knew certain cooked vegetables I could have and fish, and I think she talked to some of the counselors at the Macrobiotic Center about me. She told them about the bowel problem, and they told her what I could have and what to stay away from because it would be hard to digest. I started reading a lot, so instead of being frightened and worrying about cancer, I became obsessed with reading the macrobiotic books, going to the store and buying more books. I threw myself into it. It wasn't peach pits, so Gene started listening to me talk about it, and he thought, *Well, this isn't too bad. I'll support this.*

The more research I did, the more I found out I had to change. You had to have a gas stove to cook macrobiotics and we had an electric stove. So I had Grace have gas put in outside and I bought a new gas stove and put the electric stove in the garage. I decided to eat the macrobiotic way. Grace was filling shelves with foods she'd never seen in her life—whole grains, seaweeds and tofu. I met other people on macrobiotics and they were very encouraging. Nobody said to me, "Don't have your chemo." What they said was, "Do this too. Clean your body out. It's going to take time." Gene was happy because I was no longer a bomb about to explode. I was able to sleep better at night. I'd get up in the morning and make miso soup and study cookbooks. I had been in such desperate straits that this became the panacea. I could get up in the morning. I could live.

A week later I went into New York and I had a meeting with one of the very best macrobiotic counselors. You go in and fill out forms about your condition and pay quite a lump of money to see a counselor for an hour. He assesses you through looking at your face and feeling your hands. He uses diagnostic procedures based just on looking at and touching your body. Then he gives you food recommendations for what you're going through. The counselor knew about my radiated bowel so he prescribed a food program that took that into account. He also knew I was going through chemo. After he examined me and read what I'd written about my case, he looked at me and said, "You have a chance to recover." That was the best news I'd heard in forever. All I could see in the Connecticut oncologist's face was that he didn't believe I would recover. He seemed to have no hope for me, and I had no faith in him. But this macrobiotic counselor said I had a chance to recover and all I had to do was cook miso soup a certain way on my gas stove and eat rice cream five or six times a day and eat certain root vegetables and carp soup four days on and three days off—very specific, very balanced, which is important in the macrobiotics philosophy. The macrobiotic diet consists mostly of whole grains like brown rice, supplemented by certain vegetables and beans, but I couldn't have the beans or the vegetables because of my intestines—too much fiber. The counselor told me to have patience.

I had dinner that night at the Macrobiotic Center and heard a lecture by a woman doctor who was very inspiring. I drove back with the woman who had been helping me. I began to see her as "the Angel of Life" because she had golden red curly hair, and when light shone through it she glowed. She was cooking for me. She was saying I could get well—if I ate this food, I could get well. "Think of the food as medicine," she said.

I knew that more chemotherapies were coming up and I wasn't going to be able to cook for myself. The Angel of Life had a family and wouldn't always be able to make me food. So I called the Macrobiotic Center in New York and told them that I would like to hire someone to come and cook for me. They sent a young man, an Italian named Anthony. He came and lived with us and our new gas stove. Anthony was cooking just for me; all the others had to fend for themselves.

There was always the smell of fish in the kitchen and

there were always bowls of mysterious beans and seeds and grains. Anthony was a very healing cook, a very bright man. He had owned a vegetarian restaurant in Europe and was about a year older than me. He was very much into macrobiotics, a very controlled, balanced person. He would do t'ai chi outside every day and swim and walk peacefully through the garden.

As only I can, I went bonko, completely nutty. I did everything macrobiotically. They said wear only cotton clothes, so I threw out all my clothes that were blends. No jewelry, they said, so I took off all my jewelry—my rings, my earrings, everything. No nail polish. I changed all my cosmetics to natural products, because they also recommended that. I had loofah sponges and body scrubbers and herbal soaps and seaweed toothpaste. I went to health-food stores and bought everything in the macrobiotic section. Anthony was my personal and private cook, but he also spoke to me all the time about healing. He would take me outside and have me walk in my stocking feet on the stones in the driveway to help my intestines. He would run me through t'ai chi. He would tell me that I was too nervous, that I spoke on the phone too much, so I decided I would never speak on the phone again. Grace and Gene were instructed just to tell people I didn't speak on the phone. I wouldn't even talk to Judy. She would call all the time but I wouldn't speak to anyone—the phone was a drain on my energy. I decided I was not going to answer any more of my mail, either, that it was also draining me. I had my own fight to fight now. I continued having my Wednesday meetings, although people didn't come so often—sometimes only one person would show up. There really was no one to run the group, no therapist or anybody with an overview. I was focused only on myself now that I'd become macrobiotic.

Anthony said it would be better for my intestines if I took my meals by myself and chewed them thoroughly. Everything was pureed for my intestines. He would make me certain kinds of fish and pureed vegetables. He was always cooking wonderful things and grinding them down to something I could digest. I always ate by myself. No one was allowed to come near me when I was eating. I'd get to chewing so much that I'd go into little reveries of chewing. I'd look at the trees and appreciate my life and be humble. That's the attitude of macrobiotics, to be humble and to appreciate. Breakfast was almost always miso soup or rice cream, but before breakfast I'd be walking barefoot on the dew in the flowing cotton clothes. Anthony said, "Before breakfast you must walk in bare feet in the fresh dew on the grass." Whatever Anthony said, I did.

Anthony would give me lectures during the day about the macrobiotic philosophy of life. He said that *macrobiotic* means "great life" or "long life." He would say my trouble was that I would go all the way to the extreme of happiness, then I would go all the way to the extreme of despair. If I lived a life more balanced, more in the middle, emotionally, then I would be more likely to get well. He wanted me not to get so happy that I wouldn't get so sad, to stay calm above everything else—to go to bed earlier and get up earlier. He thought I should plant a garden and be in balance with nature.

In the meantime, I was losing about a pound a day

because there was no fat in my diet. When I went to see the Connecticut oncologist that first time I weighed about 116 pounds. During my macrobiotic stage, I went down to 93 pounds. I just got thinner every day. Gene was happy I was getting out of bed in the morning, working on my book and less fearful. But Grace didn't know what to do—every time she opened the fridge, there'd be some weird-smelling thing in there. Grace has lived a lot of years and seen a lot of things but not one of these foods had she seen before. Ours used to be this happy house where we'd have tuna and coleslaw and lettuce and tomatoes every day for lunch and the house would be brimming with tastes and flavors. Now there were only bean curd and little packages of miso paste in the fridge. In fact, there was one thing that smelled so bad I couldn't believe it—some kind of fermented soybeans. Anthony said, "Oh, you'll develop a taste for it." I never did.

The two carboplatin treatments had taken their toll on my energy. And I felt a noticeable increase in the numbness in my hands and feet. When I went to see the Connecticut oncologist, I had this conversation:

"I notice that I'm having more numbness in my hands and feet. I hope I don't have to go to a neurologist again."

He said, "Well, what would be the point?"

"What do you mean?"

"You have no choice."

I said, "Oh."

He said, "You have to have these treatments anyway, and I want to tell you you're very brave to face what could happen."

I wanted to strangle him. What kind of talk was that? Telling me I had no choice. I don't know why he was so hostile to me.

The last straw came a week later when I went to his office to have a blood transfusion. The chemo nurse hooked me up so a pint of my donor's blood would go through my Port-A-Cath. After about an hour she realized the blood wasn't going through very quickly. She thought she'd better test my Port-A-Cath so she tried to wash it through with saline.

"Oh, this is clogged. Your Port-A-Cath is clogged."

I said, "No, it can't be."

She said, "Well, sometimes the vein gets clogged up or something. Listen, we'll give you an IV in your arm to get the blood."

I said, "No, I don't want to be stuck. It's more painful."

She said, "Well, we'll just have to. Don't worry, we'll just stick you once."

I agreed.

So I got a transfusion in my arm while she kept testing the Port-A-Cath. She injected a special solution to try to unclog any blood in it. Nothing happened. Then the Connecticut oncologist came in, and she said, "Her Port-A-Cath is clogged." They started talking about me as though I wasn't even in the room.

He said, "Well, *she'll* have to have a new Port-A-Cath put in. Let's put *her* in the hospital now and we'll have them run a dye study to see if it's clogged or not."

Then the nurse said, "No, let's give *her* the weekend."

I'm sitting right there through all this while they're deciding on my life.

"All right, we'll give *her* the weekend."

They finished giving me the blood and I came home. Gene was playing tennis; Anthony was watching soccer on TV. I was only home an hour when I started to run a fever from the stuff that had been put through the Port-A-Cath.

I said to Gene, "I will never go back there again. I will not see that doctor again. He is death to me. He looks at me and he sees me dying. He's just doing what's necessary until I die. I'm going to stay on my macrobiotics. I believe in it. I don't want to deal with the medical community anymore. I don't like the way they're handling me. I don't care if my Port-A-Cath works. I'm not having any more chemotherapy anyway. I'm finished. I don't want to call him. You can help me out by calling him and telling him that I'm no longer his patient."

Gene said, "Well, I'd like you to have an oncologist, Gilda. I understand what you're saying, but I feel you should still be seeing someone."

I said, "I don't want to and I don't need to. This is fine with me."

Gene was wonderful. He called the Connecticut oncologist, and he said exactly what I had said: "Gilda says she no longer wishes to be your patient because she doesn't feel you see her as recovering."

They had their conversation and then Gene came back and reported to me.

I asked Gene, "Did he say he *did* see me as recovering?"

Gene said, "Well, no, but he did say 'I understand' and got off the phone."

Then I was upset because I thought, *He* really *thinks I'm going to die!* Within ten minutes, the phone rang, and it was the Connecticut oncologist calling back. He said to Gene, "I want you to know that I do feel she can get well. I feel that she has to be patient, and there are a lot of treatments and different things we can do, but I feel she can get well."

Gene said, "Well, thank you, but Gilda would prefer not to be with your practice."

That was that. I was glad that he had at least had the sensitivity to call back.

I settled into my new life without oncologists. I had Anthony. He was my closest companion. He was the only one I made laugh. I didn't talk to anybody else, and Gene went out to dinner at the neighbors' house to be with people. I didn't want my neighbors to come over because they asked too many questions about macrobiotics. They kept saying, "Well, if macrobiotics can cure cancer, how come we haven't heard more about it? How come there isn't more documentation?" My girlfriend Judy was going out of her mind in Toronto waiting for me to call her. She couldn't believe I would disconnect from her totally. She decided she'd just come at the end of June for my birthday. So she made reservations for herself and her husband and her baby and my girlfriend Pam at a hotel twenty minutes from my house. She thought, *We'll just go to the hotel and let Gilda know we're twenty minutes away if she wants to see us. If she doesn't want to see us, that's okay.*

Gene didn't like the idea of my not being seen by a doctor. He proceeded to search for another oncologist. He said he had to do it for himself. He just wasn't at peace with my decision. He still believed in the medical community. Gene's sister had been through cancer, and her New York oncologist helped Gene track down someone I called the "All-New, Improved Connecticut Oncologist." But I wasn't interested.

Instead, I added another layer to the macrobiotics. The Angel of Life had given me another book called *You Can Fight for Your Life* by a psychologist named Lawrence LeShan. Joanna had talked about him at The Wellness Community as one of the forerunners of the theory of psychoneuroimmunology, using the mind to help the body heal or stay well. He had worked with hundreds of terminal cancer patients and he said that the ones who got well were the ones who were willing to change. He had had many successes with people who were psychologically willing to make great changes and would end up surviving what was considered a terminal illness. He lived in New York and I was lucky enough to get an appointment to see him. I saw him every week or ten days when he was in New York. We had deep and wonderful talks and he encouraged me to fight for my creativity and to love my own uniqueness. He was also interested in psychic healing, and I attended two healing sessions in upstate New York. Larry said that going to the sessions was like eating chicken soup—it might not help, but it couldn't hurt.

Every day I got thinner and thinner, but I was tremendously calm. I wore the cleanest, fresh cotton clothes in which I was wasting away. I didn't look too bad in my face and I still had my hair. Gene meanwhile was talking with this All-New, Improved Connecticut Oncologist he had found. I was in outer space—feeling pure, chewing my food, blessed by God, sure that I had cancer under control and that it was disappearing from my body. I was not aware that according to my last blood test, my CA-125 had risen to 245.

16.

Change

When Gene and I got married in the south of France in September of 1984, we spent the week before our wedding at our favorite château. We liked to play tennis at ten or eleven in the morning before the sun got too hot. One morning we looked out from our little villa and there was a couple on the only tennis court, playing singles at the time we most liked to play. We stood there in shock—Well, who are they? Did they sign up for the court? What right do they have to play at our favorite time? We called the concierge. He said these people had signed up every day for the next four or five days for that time on the tennis court. We spent that day being angry about it and playing our tennis in the scorching hot sun. The next day we took a chance. We put on our tennis clothes, walked down there and asked the other couple if they'd be interested in playing doubles. They said sure.

They were an older couple. The man had a slight limp and couldn't move a lot, but his shots were great. His wife was an excellent player, quite a bit taller than he was and very athletic. The four of us made for a good game. The fact that I'm such a bad player made up for the fact that the man couldn't move fast. We had a great time and decided we'd play every day. Every morning at ten o'clock, we were out there in a heated game of doubles. After the fourth day, because they were going to leave, we actually sat down to talk. The man would call Gene and me Jim and Gail. He just never heard our names right, and we never corrected him. We all sat down to have some water after playing. They asked us, what did we do? Gene said, "I'm in movies," and I said, "I'm in television."

They had never seen either of us. We were Jim and Gail, until we said that we were Gene and Gilda. Then the woman spoke up and said, "My husband and I aren't in the kind of work where we get to see a lot of entertainment."

She owned an antique store and traveled a lot.

"The reason we're here is that my husband is being honored next week in Paris for his work in chemotherapy."

They introduced themselves, Dr. and Mrs. Ezra Greenspan. In the sixties, Dr. Greenspan developed many of the protocols of multiple chemotherapy used today. Back then, doctors would give one-drug chemotherapy, but Greenspan experimented with multiple-drug therapy. They said he was nuts, but he pursued his research, and now it is standard treatment for breast cancer. You don't get one drug, you get a mixture of drugs. He is called "the father of chemotherapy." We asked Dr. Greenspan about Gene's sister, who was going through chemotherapy and radiation therapy for breast cancer, and he said to tell her to make sure she finished her year of chemotherapy. "It's very important she finishes the course, the modality of treatment." Then they left and went on to Paris. I remember we told Gene's sister about it, but I didn't think much about Dr. Ezra Greenspan until I got cancer myself.

After I was almost finished with my treatments in California, friends of ours who knew the Greenspans in New York told me Dr. Greenspan had heard that I had cancer and had said to these people, "If Gilda ever wants to call me, please let her know that I'd be glad to talk to her." At the time, I had so many doctors and I was on the West Coast and he was in New York. I didn't call him but I had his number. It remained on my list of things to do for months and months. But he didn't come up again until the *Life* magazine article came out. About a week after it was on the stands, he wrote to me and sent me a copy of *Cope* magazine because he was on the cover of it. In it was an article about his work with breast cancer and his interest in the field of immunology. He said in his letter, "We are doing great work in the control and management of ovarian cancer and when you're back East, if you're feeling up to it, my wife and I would love to play tennis again."

I wrote him back and said, "I want you to know that

after all this treatment I've been through, I still play tennis as badly as I did before and we'd love to meet with you sometime."

That was the extent of our correspondence. I remember showing the letter to Gene and saying to him, "Why did he say 'control and management of ovarian cancer,' why didn't he say 'curing ovarian cancer'?"

Gene said, "Well, you know, doctors don't want to stick their necks out and say that they can absolutely cure something."

That appeased me. Poor Gene spends half his life responding to the meanings I make up for things. I still kept Ezra Greenspan's name and phone number on my list of things to do.

By mid-June, in beautiful Connecticut, I was heavily into the macrobiotic way of life. I had to learn a whole new language of food—*umeboshi plum* was a condiment, *gomashio* were ground sesame seeds and *nori* was a kind of seaweed. There was a drink called *sweet kuzu*. It filled my brain. I'd have days when I was depressed and couldn't get out of bed or I wouldn't feel good. Anthony would come up and stand by my bed and give me health lectures about what I needed in terms of food and attitude. Gene was happy to have some of the responsibility lifted off his shoulders. It's a pain in the neck to have somebody who's worried about dying around—the whole house gets gloomy. In the weeks after my recurrence, before my macrobiotics, we would try to go out to dinner with people, but I couldn't eat because of the lump of fear in my throat. I would just stare off and the other people would be eating. Because my delight was gone, I kept thinking, *Why are they talking, how can they be enjoying themselves and drinking and order-ing this food?* I was in the black, deep, dark hole, really depressed. But it wasn't even depression, it was just tre-mendous fear and anger. So the compulsiveness of mac-robiotics was soothing. I needed it so badly, and I was glad to find someone like Anthony to be with me, willing to talk about it day and night.

I was sitting at my desk one day, I think it was a Mon-day, and Gene came in and said, "I just spoke to the All-New, Improved Connecticut Oncologist and he says he really would like to see you."

I said, "Well, I'm not going to see him, but since you're so busy making phone calls everywhere, why don't you call this number?" I handed him the paper with Ezra Greenspan's name and number on it.

He said, "All right, I will," and he disappeared into his office while I went outside to walk on pebbles in my bare feet.

A little later Gene called to me. He was excited. "Come in here, come in here. I want you to talk to Dr. Green-span, he's on the phone."

I said, "I don't want to."

"Just talk to him, Gilda. Just get on the phone and listen."

I got on and he said, "Gilda." He has a gruff voice and sounds like Mel Brooks, a real fast New York accent. "Gilda, listen to me, listen to me. You're doing the wrong thing, you're on the wrong thing. You shouldn't be on carboplatin. You've had enough of that, you don't need it. You're going to be fine, you're going to be okay. You have to get on a mixture of drugs. You have to get on methotrexate, Adriamycin, 5-FU. We put you on a mixture of drugs, we build you up a little bit with testosterone, get the bone marrow cooking. You're going to be fine. We'll get the CA-125 down to a little smidgen of a thing, then build you up. You'll be playing tennis in no time."

He fast-talked like a car salesman.

"It's no problem. I got fifteen women now with the same thing as you—the recurrence and everything—and they're doing great."

I said, "I don't want to be sick from chemo."

He said, "You've already had the worst. Just come into the office, would you please just come into the office this Thursday or Friday? Just come in."

He caught me up.

I said, "Thursday?"

He said, "That's terrific. Three o'clock, three o'clock," and he hung up the phone.

Gene came in and his eyes were all wide as though he was thinking my whole personality would now change. He was excited, but I just turned around and walked out.

I said, "I'm supposed to go in Thursday, I have an appointment with him."

Gene held back everything he was thinking and just said, "Okay."

I said to him, "I'm not going on chemo again, I'm done with chemo. He's just listing a whole lot of other poisons for me to take and it's going to be hell."

All I could think of was losing my hair again, and becoming debilitated and so on and so forth.

"But what did you think about what he said? That the carboplatin was wrong, and everything?"

I said, "I don't know and I don't care."

On Thursday, when Gene and I went in to see Greenspan, I weighed about ninety-five pounds. I had lost so much weight and I was very weak because of the macrobiotic diet and the effects of the carboplatin on my bone marrow. Dr. Greenspan's office was on Fifth Avenue in Manhattan. It was crammed with people. I looked at them all real closely to see what they looked like and who had on wigs. A lady went by in a wheelchair who had real short hair and she was blown up like a balloon, obviously on steroids. I just shuddered at everything. I wanted to go back to my macrobiotic life. We went in and there was Dr. Greenspan, whom I hadn't seen in four years. His face was open and sweet. He *still* had trouble remembering Gene's name. We brought all my medical records for him to look at. He went over them, real fast—he does everything real fast.

Then he said, "I want to examine you. Let me see, first I've got to see what kind of cell it was."

We brought my CAT scan and X-rays. He had a radiotherapist and X-ray machine right in his office. There was nothing fancy about the office. It was crowded and laid out horribly, piled with books and with all his awards on the wall. If I asked him something, he would say, "Look at that document on the wall, it says my research on yadah, yadah shows this."

He's a bit of an egomaniac, but also very specific. He looked at my records and said, "Okay, we're in luck. It's the right kind of cell. I'll tell you, you get on this program. You're going to start off with one drug and you're going to have chemo every week. Once a week or every ten days starting with 5-FU, then with 5-FU and methotrexate, then every third week with 5-FU, methotrexate and Adriamycin."

I said, "I don't want to take Adriamycin because of the heart damage."

He said, "You're going to take Adriamycin, you're going to take it. I'm not going to give you that much, I'm going to watch it. I got a lady eighty years old, she's the only one who's had a little heart damage from it. I'm going to monitor it, I'm going to watch it, I'm not going to give you more than you can take."

He was such a character that it was like going to see Mel Brooks or Willy Wonka for a medical opinion. He sounded like the Wizard of Oz did when he was selling himself. Gene was pleased; he was suppressing a smile.

Gene and I had been living with my fifteen-percent chance of survival on carboplatin. So suddenly Gene said to Greenspan, "What are the chances that this will work?"

Greenspan immediately answered, "Eighty-five percent, with a little luck. Let me examine you."

He took me in the examining room, gave me an overall exam, a pelvic and a rectal exam and felt around my lymph nodes.

"You're too thin, you've got to eat more."

I told him about my bowel problem and he said, "Well, eat anyway. Eat soup, eat juice from meat."

He wanted me to build myself up. He didn't tell me to stop the macrobiotics, but he said I had to add more protein to my diet. Before I knew it his nurse, Heather, was giving me a shot of testosterone, the male hormone, which helps to build the bone marrow, and a B_{12} shot to build up my red blood cells. Heather is an eleven-year survivor of leukemia. She still gets chemo once every four months. She's Australian and a ball of fire.

"We'll have you bouncin' aroun' in no time."

Suddenly a little door opened inside me. I had been closed in a room of anger and fear. I'd shut myself off from the real world, buried myself in magic thinking. Now, a little door just cracked open, and once again there was a chance that I could live without being on macrobiotics, that I could laugh again, and that I could eat vanilla cake with vanilla icing and maybe have a cheeseburger or do something with my girlfriend Judy. I didn't have to be isolated anymore. The comedienne inside me peeked through the little door and thought about making people laugh again. Ezra Greenspan was pulling on that door from the other side saying, "If you just come through here, if you'll have this chemotherapy, everything can be okay."

He was so positive, he was offering me hope. He said, "I'm going to treat you like my own daughter."

Well, there were the magic words. Somebody who once saw Dr. Greenspan said he had a mashed-potato face—a face you want to kiss. He said, "This will work," and then he talked about building up my immune system with certain medications in order to fight the cancer.

I asked, "How long do I have to be on the chemo?" and he said, "Two months, three months every week, then once every three weeks, and then maybe maintenance doses for a few years."

"Will I lose my hair?"

"I don't know," he answered, then made a face as if to say, "What are you talking about your hair for when we're talking about your life?"

I said, "I don't want to be nauseous."

"What is being nauseous if you get your life at the end?"

His replies reminded me of a cantankerous rabbi. I said I wanted to do my television show and he said, "By January you'll be okay to do it. You hair might not be exactly what you want it to be."

I said, "When I had this CAT scan in Connecticut, the Connecticut oncologist said to me, 'You have these nodules in your abdomen, there's a shadow on your lung, there are spots on your liver.' He said he could give me chemo and it was treatable, but he implied that I only had a few years."

Dr. Greenspan just laughed. He laughed as if to say, "What a crock of shit!" He made me retake the chest X-ray—there was *no* shadow on my lung. He said the cells were *on* my liver, not *in* my liver—and there was a big difference. He was talking about restoring my future, not just prolonging my life. He was giving me an eighty-five-percent chance at the whole potatoes, at life.

Greenspan wanted to give the first chemo right then. He said, 'It's nothing, this 5-FU, you won't have any reaction—let's give it to you today."

I said no. I wasn't ready yet. So it was agreed that the All-New, Improved Connecticut Oncologist that Gene had found and whom I'd never met would administer the chemo to me in Connecticut through Greenspan's orders the next week.

Gene was giggling all the way home in the car because he was so happy about how this had gone. We came home and we told Grace and she was happy, too. I think her ambition was to get Anthony out of the kitchen. Anthony said in his very even, balanced way that he thought it was a good idea to hear a doctor say this could happen and he thought he could balance the food in such a way to make the chemo much easier for me to take, although he said he didn't know a lot about chemo and what that did to the system, but he wanted to learn. He was very kind and understanding about it. I thought to myself, *Well, now I'll have two things attacking the cancer, this chemo and the macrobiotics.*

The first treatment caused some vomiting and some irritation of my esophagus. Of course I still had a partial bowel obstruction. A week later when I had the second treatment, which was two drugs, I had some more vomiting and more irritation so it became even more difficult to eat.

The chemo made the macrobiotic food taste terrible to me. I craved more salt. The bland food tasted so horrible that I'd gag when I looked at it. Finally, I stopped eating it.

At the same time, it was my forty-second birthday at the end of June. Judy and her husband and baby and my girlfriend Pam were camped out twenty minutes from the house. They had been there for two days. I had said I didn't want to see them, but I got sentimental and changed my mind. It was like some of my life was coming back. They looked at me and said, "Gilda, you've got to eat." I was thin and pale and weak. They convinced me to have a hamburger. It tasted delicious. My neighbors invited us all over for my birthday and Grace made me a white cake with white frosting from scratch. That was the end of macrobiotics. Anthony had to go back to New York. But he wasn't upset; he understood that things had changed. I no longer needed a macrobiotic cook. Everyone agreed that the most important thing was that I eat something—anything—because I was so thin. Everyone

—including Anthony—was interested in getting me well again. But even though I went off the macrobiotic diet, which was too strict for me now, I'd learned a great deal about the importance of balanced nutrition in treating and preventing illness. And most important, I had taken action against the disease.

I was back on intensive chemotherapy every week. But my partially obstructed bowel was continually irritated by the therapy. I had begun my treatments severely under-weight and dehydrated—in fact, almost at the point of starvation. I needed blood transfusions, and my CA-125 had risen to 245. The All-New, Improved Connecticut Oncologist got a Connecticut gastroenterologist in on my case and they wanted me to go into the hospital for a while to go on intravenous feeding to build up my strength.

I was emphatically opposed to that. No hospital. To me that seemed like the beginning of the end. Fortunately, this oncologist knew that there was a group of licensed intravenous nurses who had their own business called Home Intravenous Therapy. Medical patients could have intravenous food or antibiotics or chemotherapy at home because these four women were licensed to come and set things up and put in IVs or access a patient's Port-A-Cath at home. They were on call twenty-four hours a day. They did this service because they realized a lot of people are in the hospital unnecessarily.

So early in July, Joy and Linda and Louise and Cindy came to work for me. They ordered all the things I needed in the house: the IV pole, the pump to power the intravenous tube, all the medical supplies I needed. At night I was put on food supplements intravenously through my Port-A-Cath. Just the way Jodi was there for me in California, these four miraculous, salt-of-the-earth women appeared just when I needed them. They were wonderful nurses, very near my own age and all married and raising families. They were able to draw my blood at home, take it to the lab and call in the results to my doctors. Everything was set up so I didn't have to go to any doctor's office and I didn't have to go to any hospital. Each of the four nurses would come on a different day.

The All-New, Improved Connecticut Oncologist was a good doctor, kind and compassionate. He gave me my chemos through my Port-A-Cath at home once a week, every Monday or Tuesday. Then whichever nurse was available would come too. They called it "the chemo party." Those nurses would make me laugh, or they'd dance around the bed and entertain me. They also got me to wear an ice cap on my head to help save my hair. It's a weird-looking sort of helmet that cools the skin and blood vessels in the scalp and inhibits the flow of chemical-laden blood to that part of the body. The chemo parties were like the scene in *Cinderella* when the little birds and the mice come to wake Cinderella up in the morning. One minute you think her life's so bad, but then she has all these little friends. That's what I felt like.

Gene was committed to doing a movie with Richard Pryor that was to begin shooting in August in the New York area. He hadn't worked during all of my illness, and we both knew it was important he take this job. But in

July he was exhausted from our months of uncertainty, and he needed a vacation. He decided to go to the south of France for ten days. Grace stayed with me and I had the IV nurses, plus my girlfriends Judy and Pam, who came back for extra loving care.

But while Gene was away, I became terribly ill. I began to throw up all the time. I couldn't hold down any food at all. The chemo was making my bowel obstruction worse. The bowel was closing to the point where I had an almost complete obstruction. Not only could my intestines not absorb food, they couldn't even absorb the natural secretions that my body produced. Bile would accumulate until I became nauseous and had to throw up. I could not eat. Only the intravenous feedings and fluids at night kept me alive. My bedroom looked like a hospital room. I was so weak from chemotherapy that I had to have four blood transfusions. It was the most frightening episode in my entire illness, and I thought I wasn't going to make it. I was so sick that I couldn't even tell what was going on. I didn't know whether the chemo or the obstruction was making me sick. And because this happened during those ten days when Gene was away, I confronted my biggest fear: the fear of abandonment. I discovered that even with Gene away, there were people to love and support me.

Greenspan knew I had the obstruction, but he had to bring the cancer back under control before I could have surgery to open my intestines. Greenspan conferred with the doctors in Connecticut and decided to continue the chemo while giving me my nutrition through the IV at night. I was caught in a never-never land of hope and faith and something—maybe a miracle. As awful as all of this was, I didn't become depressed. I was scared, but things were so horrible that I didn't dare give into depression. During the worst of it I remember sitting up and saying, "I'm not going to give up. I'm going to fight." I had the four nurses and my girlfriends Judy and Pam helping me. And Grace was always there, keeping everything under control. One nurse, Joy, used to come over every day just to make sure I'd get out and drive in the car or do something. Another nurse, Linda, always found the time to talk to me about cancer philosophy and fear. All four nurses became my friends and enriched my life. They made me get dressed and washed every day. It was still summer and beautiful and sometimes I'd sit on the back porch in a chair and just stare. I didn't have the energy to do anything. I couldn't eat or even drink because I would just throw up. When I felt really hungry, I would take the food in my mouth and chew it, and then spit it out into a napkin, just to have the taste. But as the chemotherapy continued, my taste buds changed and I lost interest in doing even that.

By the time Gene came back, I was out of the most desperate part of the situation. I was very thin still, but I looked better—more color in my cheeks and more confidence that I would get well. My hair was thinning and my eyelashes were falling out, but otherwise I looked all right. My face was rounding out from the low doses of steroids I was on with the chemo. Because of the testosterone, I began to grow a little mustache and hairs on my chin. I bleached everything blond and complained to Greenspan, "What are you doing to me?"

And he'd get that look on his face that said, "We're talking about your life, what's a beard and a mustache? You won't have that forever."

So I had hair falling out of my head and growing on my face at the same time.

Everything continued this way—nighttime feedings and vomiting during the day—through July and August and September. I continued to get chemotherapy just about every week. The time in between would go so fast that I couldn't believe it. All of a sudden it would be chemo day again and I'd be nervous. But the nurses would come and cheer me up, being really positive, talking about getting well and how the chemo was working. And there were more good signs—I was putting on weight and I was looking better and stronger.

What do you do when you don't eat? When I got up in the morning I didn't have breakfast, not even anything to drink. Instead I got interested in catalogues, sending away for stuff. In fact, I became obsessed with catalogues. Beside my bed I had stacks of catalogues. When I got up in the morning, the first thing I did was go through them. Then later in the day I'd send away for stuff. Within about ten days, things started arriving in the mail—all kinds of things: stamps with my name on them and a scarf that had real hair bangs attached to it in the front and an umbrella with musical notes on it and a talking picture frame. There was a Catholic high school in Joy's neighborhood that had bingo on Tuesday and Thursday nights. So after all my years in show business, I got back to the bingo table, where I really belonged. No one recognized me. I played sixteen cards at once and didn't win, but Joy won forty dollars and another nurse, Cindy, won ten dollars.

One night while Pam was with me, she and Joy and I stayed up till three o'clock in the morning. We were taping shows off the radio and dancing in the kitchen. After Joy hooked me up to my intravenous feeding, we got talking. I was doing most of the talking, about my career and my times in television, things that were really amazing that had happened in my life. Talking about all this got me excited about living, the way slumber parties did when I was a kid. I thought, *What are we doing up until three o'clock in the morning?* Joy had a family at home; this was crazy. But I joked with them about it, saying, "Sure, you two can stay up. You're not battling cancer, you'll be fine! I can't stay up this late!"

But we couldn't stop talking. There was something wonderful about it, exciting and defiant. We all enjoyed it and it made me feel that my body was turning toward life. My creative juices were flowing again. I went back to writing my book, and an amazing thing happened—I realized one day that I had my joy back. Even with all that was happening to me, I was dancing in the kitchen, I was staying up until three in the morning, I was laughing again, I was making jokes, I was going to bingo. I was enjoying my glorious life.

By September, Dr. Greenspan, my Connecticut gastroenterologist, and the All-New, Improved Connecticut Oncologist decided it was time to do something about my obstructed bowel. I had been on chemo once a week for almost three months. My CA-125 had dropped from 245 to 90. My weight was up to 114 pounds and my blood tests were pretty good. But before I could have surgery,

I had to go through a whole series of tests. I had an upper GI done, which showed the blockage was in the upper intestines. I had an MRI scan, which is similar to a CAT scan, and it showed no evidence of nodules in the abdomen and no liver problem. I had yet another barium enema, which showed no blockage in the lower bowel (I'm happy to report that the enema technique has been improved in the last two years, so it is faster and less humiliating).

On October 3, 1988, I had my third operation in three years, this time in a big hospital in New York City with a top New York surgeon and a New York gynecological oncologist in charge. They were able to repair the blockage. Biopsies and a saline wash revealed no evidence of tumor activity. I'd be able to eat again, and the Greenspan chemo program was working.

When I came out of surgery, I had a nasogastric tube in my nose and a catheter in my crotch, an intravenous feeding tube in my Port-A-Cath and a peripheral intravenous line in my arm. I went from 114 pounds to 134 pounds in two days because I was retaining fluid. Every part of me was blown up, and I spent a very uncomfortable two weeks in my room overlooking Central Park. Greenspan came to see me every day and my case was followed by what seemed like twenty-five residents and interns, who all looked to me as though they were still in high school. I couldn't have the tube removed from my nose until there were signs that my bowel was working. The indication, if you can believe it, would be that I could pass gas. After ten long days, lo and behold, I had gas! When I had a bowel movement, I called Greenspan's office to tell him. He was out so the receptionist asked, "Can I take a message?"

I said, "This is Gilda Radner. Tell Dr. Greenspan my bowels moved."

When I was sixteen years old, my girlfriend and I had gone up north to her parents' cottage. Because we went to a girls' school, we didn't see boys that much. There were a bunch of boys up north, so we invited them over. We had beer and some food, pretzels, popcorn and stuff. We were all sitting around, and the guys were cute and everything, but the girls were on one side and the boys on the other. We were telling jokes and talking and laughing and I started to laugh, and by accident I passed gas. Everyone looked at me with suppressed laughter. It was obvious where the noise had come from. I was devastated. It was a nightmare—here's one of my first times with guys and I do the most disgusting thing. What guy will ever like me? How can they even think of me romantically? Now here it was twenty-five years later, and I had all these guys *waiting* for me to fart! Waiting on the edge of their seats for me to pass wind. Here's life coming around again. All these cute, handsome residents and I say, "I passed gas today!" and they are so happy about it. I think they were even attracted to me. Greenspan was so happy he called back and said, "You made my day, you made my day!"

While I was in the hospital, I put on my robe with the World War II wings that Harold Benjamin had given me. The wings reminded me that I just happen to live in a war-torn country, which is my own body. I've had to suffer a lot of things that most people don't have to suffer.

My reward is my life and the value I now put on it. A lot of people who go through cancer and come out of it say that afterward they get up happy every morning and appreciate life. They smell the roses and notice everything. Even after all I've been through, I still have days when I don't notice anything. I can still drive to the drugstore and not notice the trees because I'm thinking about something else. I still get depressed and angry. I even had the nerve to say the other day that I don't want to live anymore. Afterward I wondered how someone who's fought so hard to live could say that, but I was just blue that day, blue because it's so hard.

Sometimes what I've been through will flash back on me and it horrifies me. I can't believe it happened to me —not me, thinking, conscious, funny Gilda, the clown. How could these things have happened? I don't have to dream or imagine it, I just have to recall that it actually happened.

Today I'm continuing a maintenance chemotherapy. I don't want to place too much faith in Dr. Greenspan as I did in other doctors, but he's done so much for me, and there's something about this cantankerous, defiant man. He talks too fast, and when I complain he says to me, "Shut up, shut up."

I just want to kiss him because he believes that I will get completely well, and I think sometimes that has even more to do with how much the chemo works than what a doctor chooses to give you. I know better now that fighting cancer is a continuing process, like controlling diabetes or any chronic disease. I have to continue to fight it. My eating habits, my lifestyle, my attitude, continuing to get treatment, building my immune system—I have to keep fighting and I can't ever stop. I can't ever let down and say, "I beat it, I licked it, I'm finished."

But mostly, I can't be afraid of cancer. What I've learned the hard way is that there's always something you can do. It may not be an easy thing to do. In some cases death seems more desirable. But there is always something you can do.

I also had to realize that I couldn't do everything I wanted to do. I couldn't keep calling all the cancer patients I knew, and I couldn't try to help heal all the women with ovarian cancer, and I couldn't read every letter I received because it was ripping me apart. I couldn't be Mother Teresa. I couldn't cry all those tears for everybody else, I had to take care of myself. For a while I thought that if I helped the world then I could get well by magic, but I learned that it just doesn't happen that way. I couldn't follow the progress of everyone I knew who had cancer because I had to pour all my energy into taking care of myself. I had to stop comparing myself to other people and thinking that what might happen to them was going to happen to me. It is important to realize that you have to take care of yourself because you can't take care of anybody else until you do.

Of course, my ordeal has been speckled with angels. I've been blessed with wonderful people. Gene didn't give up. He believed in me and never treated me like my days were numbered. I've been blessed because of advances in medical science, and I've been blessed with nurses, like Jodi, who sat in coffee shops with me in California, and the Connecticut nurses who joined me at bingo. And my girlfriends Pam and Judy, and Grace, and the fact that I've been able to afford to get the treatment that I did get, not to mention the miraculous Sparkle, a five-pound Yorkshire terrier who mimics my every mood and is my constant companion. Joanna Bull and The Wellness Community gave me the tools to be a fighter, and I have no doubt that the more I took control, and the more I participated in my health care, the more my body responded and the better I felt.

I had wanted to wrap this book up in a neat little package about a girl who is a comedienne from Detroit, becomes famous in New York, with all the world coming her way, gets this horrible disease of cancer, is brave and fights it, learning all the skills she needs to get through it, and then, miraculously, things are neatly tied up and she gets well. I wanted to be able to write on the book jacket: "Her triumph over cancer" or "She wins the cancer war." I wanted a perfect ending, so I sat down to write the book with the ending in place before there even *was* an ending. Now I've learned, the hard way, that some poems don't rhyme, and some stories don't have a clear beginning, middle and end. Like my life, this book has ambiguity. Like my life, this book is about not knowing, having to change, taking the moment and making the best of it, without knowing what's going to happen next. Delicious ambiguity, as Joanna said.

When I was little, Dibby's cousin had a dog, just a mutt, and the dog was pregnant. I don't know how long dogs are pregnant, but she was due to have her puppies in about a week. She was out in the yard one day and got in the way of the lawn mower, and her two hind legs got cut off. They rushed her to the vet and he said, "I can sew her up, or you can put her to sleep if you want, but the puppies are okay. She'll be able to deliver the puppies."

Dibby's cousin said, "Keep her alive."

So the vet sewed up her backside and over the next week the dog learned to walk. She didn't spend any time worrying, she just learned to walk by taking two steps in the front and flipping up her backside, and then taking two steps and flipping up her backside again. She gave birth to six little puppies, all in perfect health. She nursed them and then weaned them. And when they learned to walk, they all walked like her.

The day after Gilda's funeral I was going through drawers and found several sheets of colored construction paper, on which she had made a little drawing of her body and then asked herself questions. She wrote each question very clearly with her right hand and then, apparently, switched the pen to her left hand to scrawl out the answers...trying, I believe, to make contact with the child inside, without the adult Gilda censoring any of her feelings; as if she were holding the little Gilda in her arms and asking...why?

Gilda showed me the little poem in May of 1989, three weeks before she died.

Gene Wilder

Right Hand Questions—
Left Hand Answers

What are you?
I am your tummy—your stomach, your bowels.

How do you feel?
I feel cramped and clogged—not relaxed—frightened. I hate everything that tries to go through me.

What caused you to feel this way?
I have always felt this way. Not relaxed. My mother made me feel that food wasn't allowed inside. Now radiation has made my bowel all scarred.

How can I help you?
Help me to relax—to not make me afraid to eat.

You can eat. It is wonderful and nurturing.
No, cancer won't let me eat. It hurts too much, or I am nauseous with fear or from treatments.

Is cancer your mother inside you?
She doesn't want me to exist.

Well, get her out.
How?

By loving yourself—by becoming your own mother—only you can do that—love the little you—the baby, the woman.
Can I cry? I miss my mommy.

Yes, cry—but not for long—you are inside you to love you deeply—to make up for all the lost love.
Please be consistent.

What would make you not afraid?
If someone could for sure tell me that everything was going to be O.K.

How can anyone ever know for sure?
Your parents could say it.

But did they really know for sure?
No! They were just making it up.

Well why don't you make it up?
Everything is going to be O.K. Even though things seem difficult now they can't turn out to be anything but O.K.

What if my hands and feet keep getting numb?
You will adjust. You will learn to live with whatever you are left with.

Gilda's Poem

My body turned a cold back on me, at less than
    forty-three
It started a war
whatever for
in the middle of the middle of my life
it rose a black dividing mass
in my ovaries, alas
and growing fast
what was the point
a childish attempt
to eat me alive and wreck the count
my spirit strives to hold the fort
shaking its fist at each report
this is a shame, days
spending my life in bed on my back
in the middle of the middle of my life.
I can see roses in front of my hedge
with doctors pinned on their petal ledges
and nurses too and you and love and "alive" scribbled
    not far above